W9-AYQ-434

Number 126
Summer 2010

New Directions for Evaluation

Sandra Mathison
Editor-in-Chief

Enhancing Disaster and Emergency Preparedness, Response, and Recovery Through Evaluation

Liesel Ashley Ritchie
Wayne MacDonald
Editors

ENHANCING DISASTER AND EMERGENCY PREPAREDNESS, RESPONSE, AND RECOVERY THROUGH EVALUATION
Liesel Ashley Ritchie, Wayne MacDonald (eds.)
New Directions for Evaluation, no. 126
Sandra Mathison, Editor-in-Chief

Microfilm copies of issues and articles are available in 16mm and 35mm, as well as microfiche in 105mm, through University Microfilms Inc., 300 North Zeeb Road, Ann Arbor, Michigan 48106-1346.

New Directions for Evaluation is indexed in Cambridge Scientific Abstracts (CSA/CIG), Contents Pages in Education (T & F), Educational Research Abstracts Online (T & F), ERIC Database (Education Resources Information Center), Higher Education Abstracts (Claremont Graduate University), Social Services Abstracts (CSA/CIG), Sociological Abstracts (CSA/CIG), and Worldwide Political Sciences Abstracts (CSA/CIG).

NEW DIRECTIONS FOR EVALUATION (ISSN 1097-6736, electronic ISSN 1534-875X) is part of The Jossey-Bass Education Series and is published quarterly by Wiley Subscription Services, Inc., A Wiley Company, at Jossey-Bass, 989 Market Street, San Francisco, California 94103-1741.

SUBSCRIPTIONS cost $85 for U.S./Canada/Mexico; $109 international. For institutions, agencies, and libraries, $256 U.S.; $296 Canada/Mexico; $330 international. Prices subject to change.

EDITORIAL CORRESPONDENCE should be addressed to the Editor-in-Chief, Sandra Mathison, University of British Columbia, 2125 Main Mall, Vancouver, BC V6T 1Z4, Canada.

www.josseybass.com

Editorial Policy and Procedures

New Directions for Evaluation, a quarterly sourcebook, is an official publication of the American Evaluation Association. The journal publishes empirical, methodological, and theoretical works on all aspects of evaluation. A reflective approach to evaluation is an essential strand to be woven through every issue. The editors encourage issues that have one of three foci: (1) craft issues that present approaches, methods, or techniques that can be applied in evaluation practice, such as the use of templates, case studies, or survey research; (2) professional issues that present topics of import for the field of evaluation, such as utilization of evaluation or locus of evaluation capacity; (3) societal issues that draw out the implications of intellectual, social, or cultural developments for the field of evaluation, such as the women's movement, communitarianism, or multiculturalism. A wide range of substantive domains is appropriate for *New Directions for Evaluation;* however, the domains must be of interest to a large audience within the field of evaluation. We encourage a diversity of perspectives and experiences within each issue, as well as creative bridges between evaluation and other sectors of our collective lives.

The editors do not consider or publish unsolicited single manuscripts. Each issue of the journal is devoted to a single topic, with contributions solicited, organized, reviewed, and edited by a guest editor. Issues may take any of several forms, such as a series of related chapters, a debate, or a long article followed by brief critical commentaries. In all cases, the proposals must follow a specific format, which can be obtained from the editor-in-chief. These proposals are sent to members of the editorial board and to relevant substantive experts for peer review. The process may result in acceptance, a recommendation to revise and resubmit, or rejection. However, the editors are committed to working constructively with potential guest editors to help them develop acceptable proposals.

Sandra Mathison, Editor-in-Chief
University of British Columbia
2125 Main Mall
Vancouver, BC V6T 1Z4
CANADA
e-mail: nde@eval.org

CONTENTS

EDITORS' NOTES

The challenges associated with evaluating various efforts associated with disaster and emergency management are numerous and complex—arguably to an extent well beyond that of evaluations that occur in other settings. Although this is certainly not a new situation, recent large-scale domestic and international disaster events, like the January 2010 earthquake in Haiti, illuminate the matter in compelling ways. In this issue, authors provide insights from various perspectives both on the international and domestic fronts.

In Chapter 1, we provide a framework to consider the complexity of designing and conducting evaluations of disaster and emergency management. Chapter 2 examines real-time evaluation (RTE), an increasingly popular approach to evaluation in the international realm, which offers innovative ways to empower frontline disaster response staff and possibly even beneficiaries of assistance. The authors discuss the relationship between RTE and monitoring and impact assessment, and examine the utility and effectiveness of RTE in the international context of intra- and interagency efforts. Chapter 3 highlights the international trend toward interagency or joint evaluations of humanitarian response, using the Interagency Health and Nutrition Evaluation (IHE) initiative as a case study.

In Chapter 4, the authors explore the evolution of Save the Children's policy and practice with respect to evaluation utilization and learning to drive systematic improvements. They explain ways in which the organization is seeking to be more deliberate, coordinated, and accountable with respect to their efforts in this arena.

Chapter 5 offers a comprehensive evaluation framework to prepare for evaluating school emergency management programs. The authors present a framework that involves a logic model incorporating Government Performance and Results Act (GPRA) measures as a foundation for comprehensive evaluation that complements performance monitoring used by the U.S. Department of Education as part of its Readiness and Emergency Management for Schools (REMS) grant program.

Chapter 6 addresses the work of the Katrina Aid Today (KAT) consortium, created in the aftermath of Hurricane Katrina. The authors review the KAT model and examine critical aspects of implementing and adapting an interagency monitoring and evaluation system, emphasizing the role of program evaluation in disaster recovery. In Chapter 7, the authors present

---

Note: The editors would like to acknowledge Ashly Barlau of the Natural Hazards Center, University of Colorado, for her assistance compiling this issue.

NEW DIRECTIONS FOR EVALUATION, no. 126, Summer 2010 © Wiley Periodicals, Inc., and the American Evaluation Association. Published online in Wiley InterScience (www.interscience.wiley.com) • DOI: 10.1002/ev.324

1

results from an evaluation of a combination of TsunamiReady™-based educational materials distributed in New Hanover County, North Carolina. Based on their findings, the authors contend that a community's hazard experiences and the frequency and severity of hazard events play an important role in receptiveness to educational efforts as well as to participation in disaster preparedness activities. Chapter 8 provides an overview of the challenges faced by applied scholars, researchers, and evaluators when conducting disaster and crisis research. In this chapter, the authors address issues of data collection, randomization, and data analysis specifically related to disaster research. Chapter 9 summarizes key issues in disaster and emergency management evaluation, and suggests possibilities for future work in this arena.

The original call for submissions for this issue elicited 35 proposals. In reviewing these, our goal and difficult task was to select manuscripts that would to some extent capture the diversity of subjects in this very broad arena and reveal potential gaps in practice and theory. In this context, we consider the content of this volume a point of departure for future inquiry and dialogue regarding a topic that, unfortunately, has the potential to impact each of us. It is our hope that solid advances in evaluation can ultimately contribute to enhancing disaster and emergency preparedness, response, and recovery.

Liesel Ashley Ritchie
Wayne MacDonald
Editors

LIESEL ASHLEY RITCHIE is assistant director for Research at the University of Colorado's Natural Hazards Center.

WAYNE MACDONALD is director of Corporate Performance and Evaluation with Canada's Social Sciences and Humanities Research Council in Ottawa.

NEW DIRECTIONS FOR EVALUATION • DOI: 10.1002/ev

Ritchie, L. A., & MacDonald, W. (2010). Enhancing disaster and emergency preparedness, response, and recovery through evaluation. In L. A. Ritchie & W. MacDonald (Eds.), *Enhancing disaster and emergency preparedness, response, and recovery through evaluation. New Directions for Evaluation, 126,* 3–7.

1

Enhancing Disaster and Emergency Preparedness, Response, and Recovery Through Evaluation

Liesel Ashley Ritchie, Wayne MacDonald

Abstract

The authors offer a conceptual framework explicating how evaluation can enhance disaster and emergency preparedness, response, and recovery. The phases of preparedness, response, and recovery in any disaster situation are connected to who has responsibility for the evaluation and how the evaluation will be used. The complexity of the relationships among these diverse elements suggests that evaluation in this domain needs to be flexible and strategic to be beneficial. © Wiley Periodicals, Inc., and the American Evaluation Association.

Events such as the Balkan crisis and Rwandan genocide in the early 1990s, Darfur 10 years later, 9/11 in the United States, the Indian Ocean tsunami, Hurricanes Katrina, Rita, and Gustav, earthquakes in northwest Pakistan and Kashmir, cyclones Sidr (Bangladesh) and Nargis (Myanmar), and recurring emergencies in Haiti, including the January 2010 earthquake, have drawn considerable attention to disaster and emergency management. In these diverse contexts, issues of preparedness, response, recovery, and resilience are being scrutinized more closely from a variety of perspectives, highlighting a critical need for increased transparency, accountability, and learning in disaster and emergency management evaluation. At stake are millions of vulnerable people victimized by disaster, both in developed and developing countries. People should be able to rely on first responders and humanitarian assistance systems to deliver in a timely, effective, and appropriate manner, but results have often been mixed. Failures are readily reported in the media, and the challenge to aid providers is always "Do better!" This issue aims to encourage the close scrutiny of disaster and emergency management evaluation in international and domestic settings.

Surprisingly little has been written about evaluation of disaster or emergency management, although in recent years dozens of special journal issues in other disciplines have focused on disasters. In this *New Directions for Evaluation* issue, evaluators step forward and share their knowledge and experience in an effort to advance the theory and practice of evaluation in disaster and emergency settings. The authors whose work is presented in this issue represent a diverse set of individuals, organizations, backgrounds, content areas, and countries.

A Framework for Conceptualizing Disaster and Emergency Management Evaluation

Disaster and emergency preparedness, response, and recovery are complicated at the best of times, often chaotic, and driven by countless impulses and requirements. There is no precise blueprint for organizing the many facets of these activities. The respective life cycles of disaster and emergency response, performance management, and evaluation activities connect with and influence each other. It is possible to organize these many elements into multidimensional space. One way to represent this complexity is to organize the many elements into a multidimensional framework, as depicted in Figure 1.1. Each of the six sides of the cube represents attributes of disaster and emergency management evaluation. Importantly, it is not our intent to reify these attributes or this model; rather we hope that the framework will serve as common ground for dialogue and consideration of these critical issues.

Phases of Disaster and Emergency Management. Three general phases of disaster and emergency management activities (preparedness, response, and recovery) are represented in the framework on the far left side. These phases are linked to the evaluation strategy adopted, depicted at the bottom of the cube, and the extent to which evaluation efforts use an intra-agency, interagency (nongovernmental organizations, donor governments), or systemwide (United Nations) approach. Evaluation strategies are also coupled with the overall scope of an evaluation, which influences the complexity of evaluation processes. Moreover, the evaluation approaches employed are often closely tied to the physical scope of a disaster event itself, such as

Figure 1.1. Conceptual Framework for Disaster and Emergency Management Evaluation

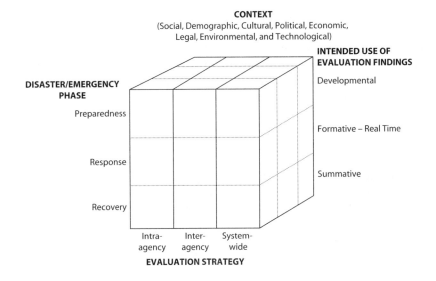

in a micro (Hurricane Katrina), mezzo (Haiti), or macro (southeast Asia tsunami) context. These reflect disasters and disaster emergency activities that take place at local, regional, national, and international levels.

Evaluation Strategy. In terms of program response, organizations can choose to respond to a disaster either from a single agency perspective, with an exclusive focus on an organization's planning, fund-raising, and operations capacity, or to coordinate their disaster emergency response with those of other organizations. The latter is increasingly becoming the norm, both within and between networks (Red Cross, United Nations, nongovernmental organizations, donor governments). Mirroring program operational response, this trend is also emerging in terms of evaluation strategy.

In the context of intra-agency evaluation strategy, a single organization, like Save the Children, might choose to limit its evaluation activities to their organization exclusively in examining performance. This would focus evaluation activities only on corporate efforts: disaster planning, emergency program operations, and other aspects of program support such as procurement, communications, finance, personnel, and informatics.

An interagency evaluation strategy might see two or more organizations, sometimes within the same network or across networks, collaborating around the evaluation strategy. One example of an interagency evaluation strategy would be the Katrina Aid Today national Case Management Consortium. On the international side, United Nations organizations such as World Health Organization, UNICEF, and World Food Program may adopt a coordinated evaluation strategy with respect to health and nutrition initiatives. Both examples enable a harmonized evaluation approach within a common context and shared intent with respect to utilization of evaluation findings. Significant economies of scale may occur with respect to framing questions, data collection, and analysis. Interagency approaches also move beyond that of a single agency to consider recommendations at a systemic level, in areas such as needs analysis, capacity building, recovery, and emergency preparedness. Such approaches may also significantly reduce organizational and respondent fatigue, although new governance challenges can emerge.

Finally, an evaluation strategy can be a collaboration between responding systems. These systemwide evaluation efforts can be very sophisticated and comprehensive, and also time consuming. One example of a systemwide evaluation was the Tsunami Evaluation Coalition (TEC), which involved the nongovernmental community, Red Cross Movement, United Nations family, and donor governments coming together to undertake a joint evaluation.

Intended Use of Evaluation Findings. The intended use of evaluation findings, shown at the far right of Figure 1.1, is an important component of the evaluation framework. We use the broad terms of developmental, formative or real time, and summative evaluation to encompass the many management functions linked to performance management (scanning, strategic planning, policy development, program design, system alignment, program implementation, monitoring and measurement, and closing and reporting processes such as audit and evaluation).

Generally speaking, each of the three aforementioned dimensions in our framework (disaster/emergency phase, evaluation strategy, and especially intended use of evaluation findings) tends to dictate or at least influence the evaluation design and methods. Broadly, the methodological paradigms are experimental or naturalistic. Regardless of the methods used, consideration must be given to issues of accuracy (validity and reliability) as well as ethical concerns in implementing an evaluation design.

Context. Finally, of critical importance is an understanding that the dimensions depicted in our evaluation framework are further influenced by the overall context in which they occur, including social, political, economic, legal, environmental, and technological factors. Failure to recognize, accommodate, and address these factors is likely to result in an evaluation that produces results that are of little use or, perhaps even worse, evaluation findings that are ultimately irrelevant to key stakeholders.

Considerations for Application of the Framework

The proposed framework is a representational device for evaluating disaster and emergency activities that is dynamic, so that evaluation is not a static undertaking. Similar to manipulating a Rubik's Cube puzzle so that each of the six colors are grouped on the same side, in order to address the challenges associated with these types of evaluation, one must keep the big picture in mind. Thus, there can and should be movement and action through time and across each of the different dimensions represented in the framework.

To be successful, the resolution of the toy puzzle mirrors emergency management response and its evaluation. It requires that one think or act not in a single move, but as a strategic collection of moves. There is no unique solution or algorithm. In any state of disarray, the cube can be solved in 22 moves or fewer. However, there is no general method for finding a solution of every variation of position. It requires planning ahead, constant monitoring, evaluating the results of a sequence of moves, and incorporating this knowledge and learning into the next set of planned moves. Simple or complex actions can sometimes require moving elements from one pre-determined place without disturbing the other attributes. The trick to solving this puzzle is that a temporary state of disorder must be produced before bringing the cube back into a state of higher order.

Reflective recall is crucial for discovering, storing, and retrieving the effects of past moves associated with solving the brain-teasing puzzle. Such is also the case for agencies involved with disaster and emergency management; corporate memory, knowledge management, measurement, and learning are critical to performance as well as evaluation. Short-term information, such as that collected in developmental, formative, and real-time evaluation, tells stakeholders where they are in the sequence of moves, and long-term information (summative evaluation efforts) relays what results from a completed series of moves. Failure to link these different stages of information can result in chaos. In terms of evaluating disaster and emergency management, this too can very quickly become complicated and, again, each action is not completely discrete. They have elements and links not only within themselves, but also with their immediate neighbors, and other layers and connections—such as the contextual factors previously described—that are not always transparent. Each of the remaining chapters in this issue examines one or more components of the matrix presented in Figure 1.1.

Liesel Ashley Ritchie is assistant director for research at the University of Colorado's Natural Hazards Center.

Wayne MacDonald is director of Corporate Performance and Evaluation with Canada's Social Sciences and Humanities Research Council in Ottawa.

New Directions for Evaluation • DOI: 10.1002/ev

2

Real-Time Evaluation in Humanitarian Emergencies

Emery Brusset, John Cosgrave, Wayne MacDonald

Abstract

The authors describe real-time evaluation (RTE) as a specific tool in disaster management and within the literature on formative evaluation, monitoring, and impact assessment. RTE offers the possibility of exploring innovative ways to empower frontline disaster response staff, possibly even beneficiaries of assistance. The authors describe conditions for the success of RTE, including field credibility, organization, and rapid analysis. © Wiley Periodicals, Inc., and the American Evaluation Association.

Real-time evaluation (RTE) is an approach increasingly invoked to generate knowledge in international humanitarian emergencies. It is defined as "an evaluation in which the primary objective is to provide feedback in a participatory way in real time (i.e., during the evaluation fieldwork) to those executing and managing the humanitarian response" (Cosgrave, Ramalingam, & Beck, 2009, p. 10). In particular, it provides a fresh view to managers and concentrates to a greater extent on the immediate effects of the intervention than normal monitoring would.

Interagency or joint RTE is also increasingly used by agencies operating in disasters, and the United Nations has commissioned a series of such evaluations (Cosgrave, Gonçalves, Martyris, Polastro, & Sikumba-Dils, 2007; Inter-Agency Standing Committee [IASC], 2006; Turner, Baker, Oo, & Aye, 2008; Young, Khattak, Bengali, & Elmi, 2007). Joint evaluation is perceived as particularly apt to study issues that cannot be studied usefully by any single agency evaluation (e.g., coordination, joint programming, gaps and balance between sectors). RTE allows for the assessment of a joint strategy even at the formative stage.

Why Are Real-Time Evaluations Necessary?

RTE refers to methods that emphasize light and mobile evaluation teams. It is focused on interactive local learning and on rapid feedback to stakeholders (either on the ground or more remote) for purposes of learning as well as of accountability. RTEs are uniquely positioned to answer the formative questions of interventions: What has been the performance so far and what is the optimal use of resources? What direction should things take? How should information be succinctly presented to mobilize resources? What stages have been reached and what should the next ones be? When and how should we begin to withdraw or begin another intervention?

Some of these questions deal not just with a valuing of what has happened, but also to an estimation of the likely outcomes of the current course of action, what the U.S. General Accounting Office (GAO) refers to as "prospective evaluation" (GAO & Datta, 1990). However, there remains no clearly defined position within the international evaluation community and among humanitarian agencies regarding the nature of RTE and the implications of key choices that RTE requires if it is to achieve its potential.

Contrasts With Other Evaluation Approaches. A review of the World Food Program's (WFP) experience with RTE notes that the complex environment and the different perceptions within the agency of what an RTE is makes RTEs arduous (World Food Program, 2004). What are the risks? To answer this question we first highlight ways in which RTE differs from other forms of performance assessments.

RTE is different from audit and inspection, mainly because of the breadth of the subject and the absence of universal standards. Both audit and inspection can be described as more or less detailed checks on the compliance of an operation to a norm that is verifiably stated in organizational, industry, or sector standards, with a focus on management structures, finances, and procurement. The aim of inspection and audit is risk reduction, and the primary purpose is accountability. RTE, on the other hand, examines the value of a result (and is hence more oriented to external standards of performance as the point of reference, even when these standards are not fully explicated) and explores the reason for achieving or not achieving those standards with a view to improvement.

RTE is distinct from other methods such as After-Action Reviews (a term coined by the U.S. Department of Defense) or Program Performance

Reviews (U.S. Office for Transition Initiatives) because of its emphasis on a broad learning perspective in the midst of a response and the systematic use of criteria-based analysis. After-Action Reviews are post hoc structured reviews or debriefings by participants and those responsible for the project or event for analyzing what happened, why, and how it can be done better. Both RTE and After-Action Review use supportive peer presence in the form of experienced facilitators cum reviewers, but After-Action Review takes place in an environment removed from the actual operation and RTE is simultaneous with program implementation. It is possible that RTEs could use After-Action Reviews as data-gathering methods.

Monitoring is usually defined in humanitarian assistance as the periodic processing of information on outputs and outcomes along a preestablished plan, most usually focused on key performance indicators. This function is performed by personnel in country or close to the operation, and supports project reporting. RTE is, on the other hand, an occasional tool, carried out by persons external to the operation. Even though they may be agency employees, these individuals are not usually involved in the implementation structure for reasons of impartiality and use of time.

Needs assessment is obviously related to how well the population and the state are doing, and RTE is a way of assisting in that process by complementing findings. Needs assessment is often a very technical task, which can benefit from inputs provided by personnel with a more systemwide performance focus. Evaluation done in real time is a subset of more general standard humanitarian or emergency evaluation—with a particular twist, which is to capture humanitarian action as it is occurring. Guidelines on the evaluation of humanitarian action (Beck, 2006; Hallam, 1998; Organisation for Economic Co-Operation and Development, Development Assistance Committee [OECD/DAC], 1999) or evaluations conducted in conflict environments (OECD/DAC, 2008) point to the importance of the specifics of a situation (e.g., polarization of society, difficulty finding information, poorly documented planning, changes in circumstances) that require specific accommodations of methodology. RTE is confronted with the same conditions, albeit accentuated, in a short reporting time.

The more theoretical literature published to date on this subject indeed would not claim that RTE is a fundamentally new concept, but rather a codification of a particular form of formative and process evaluation. For example, RTE is defined in the OECD/DAC glossary (2002) as: "An evaluation intended to improve performance, most often conducted during the implementation phase of projects or programs. This is contrasted with process evaluation, which is an evaluation of the internal dynamics of implementing organizations, their policy instruments, their service delivery mechanisms, their management practices, and the linkages among these."

Scriven (1991) defines formative evaluation as typically conducted more than once, for in-house staff, with the intent to improve. In an informal sense, operational personnel are constantly doing formative evaluation, but this is not done with the key additional assets of independent views and systematic analysis of performance information. The formal nature of RTE, as a type of formative evaluation, stems from the accountability function of reporting back to senior management and public stakeholders on the relationship between current and optimal use of resources.

A Particular Relation to Accountability and to Learning. Learning and accountability are concepts that drive the specific choices regarding the conduct and use of evaluation. The international evaluation community and emergency organizations often see these concepts as inextricable, mingled into the very make-up of the exercise. However, learning and accountability are distinct.

With respect to learning, RTE is a useful tool to improve management decision making at all levels. The recommendations and dynamics of RTEs (for example, of discussion and conversation carried out by the evaluators, but also by stakeholders independently of the evaluators) are generally seen as more relevant for operations than a longer-term evaluation.

Accountability is also a high-profile aspect of evaluation in emergency and disaster management, mostly because of the public dissemination of reports, but also because evaluators are frequently seen as channels of information to headquarters and donors. Accountability is sometimes a constraining factor, partly for reasons of sensitivity and hence access to information (an issue to which we will return), but also because of the care that should go into developing and presenting evaluation findings. Some emphasize the need for independence of RTE (in essence those who evaluate not being the same as those who implement, and being more impartial). Others emphasize that the quest for independence and accountability should not be an obstacle to fast execution of RTEs, and that truly external review will necessarily slow down the process.

The learning function of the RTE occurs through influence on policy makers, but also has clear value for those on the ground. In these conditions the United Nations, which fielded an RTE of the Darfur operations (Broughton et al., 2006), explained that evaluation is likely to be seen by country teams as a supportive measure that can help to adjust planning and performance.

These points highlight two underlying dilemmas in RTEs. One is whether RTE should be aimed at learning at the immediate level of operations, and downward or lateral accountability (and should be decided and timed by the managers), or whether they should be triggered by bodies external to the operation for broader corporate decision making, technical programming, and accountability purposes. This has implications for the scope of work and methodology, which will be reviewed in more detail in the next section.

The second dilemma is the choice between single-agency RTEs, which present fewer constraints in the area of accountability, and joint or interagency RTEs, which provide opportunities for broader perspectives and a deeper understanding of cross-cutting needs and response regime. This implies further considerations for the steering and purpose of the RTEs, as well as validation and communication strategies. The following sections tackle these issues from different perspectives.

Methodological Issues of Real-Time Evaluations

RTE is a subset of humanitarian evaluation, which is itself a subset of development evaluation. Although the real-time format imposes some constraints, the nature of humanitarian emergencies, their normal locations, and the nature of humanitarian response also limit methodological choices. Most large-scale humanitarian emergencies take place in developing countries. The conditions in developing countries limit the use of statistical sampling from a known sample frame, as there are often no reliable sample frames of the general population. The low level of telephone coverage and the absence of standard addresses rule out many surveys.

Another constraint is the nature of international humanitarian emergencies themselves. By definition, these are sudden events and responses are essentially unplanned in strategic terms. Each element of the humanitarian community acts independently while attempting to coordinate its interventions with other actors. The lack of coordination is often highlighted in the evaluations of major responses.

Furthermore, baseline studies are usually nonexistent, making before and after comparisons impossible. Even when organizations develop plans, they repeatedly have to change them as the responding organization learns more about the context of the affected community, or what was planned becomes redundant due to actions by the government or other organizations. Thus, it is very difficult to compare actual activities against planned activities in humanitarian response, as the planned activities may change even on a daily basis.

Not only does this make impact very difficult to measure, but the chaotic jumble of international organizations makes it very difficult to attribute any observed impact to any cause. If broader aims, such as preventing outbreaks of communicable disease, are met, what are the reasons? Is this because of medical coverage, the supply of clean water, effective epidemiological surveillance, or vector control? Or, is it because such outbreaks are extremely rare in any case (Floret, Viel, Mauny, Hoen, & Piarroux, 2006)? If an impact is attributed to a particular intervention, then which of the organizations working on that intervention is most responsible?

The aforementioned issues mean that humanitarian evaluation largely relies on a range of (predominantly qualitative) methods including key informant interviews, document research, discussions with communities, and occasional surveys. Although surveys are used in some specific areas of humanitarian response such as nutrition, their use in general evaluation of humanitarian response is fairly limited. Notably, the use of this method increased after the December 2004 Indian Ocean tsunami response. (See Spence & Lachlan, this issue, for a discussion of strategies for using survey methods in the evaluation of disaster relief.)

RTEs in the early stage of humanitarian response, that is, when they have the greatest opportunity to influence the overall humanitarian response, bring additional constraints. Four constraints specific to real-time humanitarian evaluation in the early stages of an international response are as follows:

1. The heavy workload on humanitarian staff dealing with the response leaves them little time for the evaluation team.
2. There is a lack of analytical documentation available at the early stage.
3. The field work needs to begin quickly to be most useful.
4. The time for analysis is limited.

The time limit for the data analysis arises as the usual intent to provide a draft report before leaving the field or at least a thorough briefing for the team implementing the humanitarian response.

Surveys in the early stages are very difficult because of the lead time needed to develop, translate, and test survey instruments, and because of the time needed to train enumerators. This preparation time effectively rules them out from use in early-stage RTE. Also, document review tends to be limited by the descriptive nature of documents. Although a later humanitarian evaluation may be able to utilize a wide range of documents in the analysis, documents in the initial stages tend to be descriptions of the ongoing response and of the intent of the responding agency. However, even at the early stages there may be a very large number of available documents. These can be a rich source for some types of analysis (including the presence of particular terms or key words in the documents) or the balance between the volume of documents from different types of actors.

Some of the questions that may be asked of an RTE relate to making assessments on likely outcome of current policies, a form of prospective evaluation. The General Accounting Office (1990) provides a useful model for evaluators making such an assessment. This model, presented in Figure 2.1, depicts the relationship between conceptual, empirical, and operational elements of a prospective evaluation.

Evaluators can only make a prospective evaluation of current policies in an RTE if they have knowledge not only of the underlying concepts, but also of the operational constraints within the agency, and of the history of such interventions. Thus, although evaluators are sometimes asked to make prospective judgments in RTEs, they should refrain from doing so unless they are confident in understanding all aspects of this triad.

Specifics of Data Collection. As with humanitarian evaluation generally, the main method used for the collection of information in humanitarian

Figure 2.1. The Triad of Analysis for Prospective Evaluation

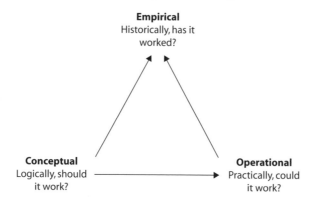

RTE is the semistructured key-informant interview that is analyzed in terms of salient themes. In the humanitarian context, such interviews are conducted with key informants purposively selected because they are "information-rich" individuals (Patton, 2002, p. 40). Evaluation teams may supplement their initial, purposive sampling with snowball sampling where each interviewee is asked to recommend other key informants until the accessible pool or the evaluators' time is exhausted. Snowball sampling is particularly applicable for RTEs where there is often no single contact list available.

Evaluators typically use an interview topic list for key informant interviews, which last from 45 to 60 minutes. They may work individually or in pairs to conduct the interview, which may be with individuals or small teams, and normally take notes that may be transcribed later. One constraint for humanitarian RTE is that interviewees may have to respond to urgent operational issues that limit their availability or lead to the premature ending of interviews. To cope with this, real-time evaluators need to be flexible in their scheduling and their approaches. For example, key questions may have to be asked at the beginning of an interview rather than waiting until the rapport is established. After-Action Review has been used for some humanitarian reviews (Baker, 2005). An After-Action Review is a facilitated discussion of an event that leads the participants through an analysis of what happened, why it happened, and how to sustain strengths and improve on weaknesses.

The workload on international field staff means that the evaluators must have field credibility in terms of their experience with humanitarian response. Such experience is also essential for the evaluators to make the most of the opportunity to observe the actions undertaken as part of the humanitarian response.

Interviews with beneficiary groups are an important source of information. In many development settings, people have to make a contribution for the goods or services provided by the organization. Their willingness to do so provides feedback to the organization on whether the goods and services are relevant. If they are not relevant, people will not make any contribution. By contrast, in humanitarian responses, goods and services are usually provided without any beneficiary contribution, and people will accept things that they don't need because they are free. This means that agencies may not get feedback on how useful their assistance is. This is especially true in the early stages of a humanitarian response and makes group interviews even more useful for RTE.

Group interviews usually take the form of meetings at which evaluators pose questions to a collection of anywhere from a handful to hundreds of community members. The presence of other community members acts as a social control on those responding to the questions, and others will often add their opinion if they disagree with what someone else has said. These group interviews are very distinct from focus-group discussions as defined by Krueger and Casey (2009). Focus groups require more preparation and control than can usually be achieved in RTE.

Observation is another key method in RTE. It is very valuable when the evaluation happens during the early stages of a response, as operations are at full strength and issues may be clearer than at other times. It is also important because operational staff may not have had time to analyze their own observations and internalize lessons that they can articulate during key informant interviews. Observation is a key resource for triangulation, and triangulation is the chief means by which RTEs strive for accuracy and reliability. Triangulation seeks to compare data gathered by different paths to determine how accurate and reliable a picture the data present of the situation. Triangulation can compare data from different sources, methods, areas, or evaluators.

The need for an RTE team to provide feedback before leaving the field is a significant constraint on the depth of analysis in which the team can engage. In an international humanitarian evaluation generally, the writing of a report after the fieldwork allows time for reflection and for considering the evidence to develop a deeper analysis, sometimes supported by further documentary research on specific aspects. In contrast, an RTE team must conduct its analysis before leaving the field.

One way of approaching this problem is to use a tool to organize the evidence uncovered during the evaluation to facilitate the drawing out of findings, conclusions, and recommendations. (See Table 2.1.) By explicitly linking evidence to findings, findings to conclusions, and conclusions to recommendations, such a tool can help to ensure that there is a strong chain of evidence for the evaluation's eventual recommendations.

Building a strong chain of evidence in this way increases the reliability of the information presented in the evaluation, a point made by Yin (2003) concerning case studies generally. Ideally, every evaluation finding should be supported by several different types of information, and every conclusion supported by several findings. Using such a tool also allows the evaluators to see when they have reached saturation on a particular issue. This happens

NEW DIRECTIONS FOR EVALUATION • DOI: 10.1002/ev

Table 2.1. A Tool for Linking Evidence to Recommendations

Evaluation Question/Issue	Evidence About This Issue	Finding	Conclusion	Recommendation
Evaluation question or issue emerging from the fieldwork	A concrete statement from interview, documentation, or an observation	Based on several pieces of evidence	Based on several findings	Based on one or more conclusions
		ILLUSTRATION		
Evaluation question	From interview 1 From site visit 2 From interview 3 From document 5 From community 4	Finding 1		
Evaluation issue (an issue emerging from fieldwork)	From interview 9 From interview 11 From document 7 From document 15 From interview 20 From site visit 4 From community 7 From community 9	Finding 2	Conclusion 1 (based on finding 1 and finding 2)	Recommendation 1

when new evidence on any issue continues merely to replicate previous evidence rather than to add any new depth to the issue. Identifying when you are reaching saturation on particular issues is useful for an RTE team, as it allows the team to use its time effectively to concentrate on a range of critical issues.

The Promise of Real-Time Evaluation

RTE can be seen as a practice that is both promising and increasingly popular in the international humanitarian field. However, there remains a need for considerable reflection regarding who it is for, who will control it, and how it should be carried out.

The answers will depend on the situation. As Sandison (2003) noted in her early review of the process of RTE, the main value of RTEs is through ". . . its timing and rapid feedback, and its combination of proximity to the actual programme and people with its evaluative distance and objectivity" (p. 8). This combination of an external view with the ability to influence decisions as they are made is the real attraction of RTE.

The days of formative evaluation as something limited to only one organization—a preoccupation of in-house program/project staff—may be numbered. In differentiating formative from summative evaluation, Scriven used a simple analogy when he quoted Robert Stake: "When the cook tastes the soup, that's formative; when the guests taste the soup, that's summative" (1991, p. 169). RTE blurs this distinction. Scriven (1991) cautions evaluators to avoid "loading formative evaluation with obligations that will bog it down, or expectations that will be disappointed" (p. 169). However, RTE does not entirely embrace this advice. In fact, the cook in the earlier analogy now starts to look more like a team of sous chefs, often involving the guests in the kitchen (e.g., senior management, decision makers, communications experts, external audiences, members of the affected population) to taste the soup. If not to their palate, ingredients can be changed or possibly the entire effort discarded.

As expectations mount, the RTE menu becomes more complicated. This may be reflective of the enlarged number of actors around the stove. Whatever the reason, the task of coordinating and using internal and external RTE evaluation teams becomes more challenging. Timing and rapid feedback are important considerations. Indeed, disaster management systems are expected, and even obliged, to demonstrate credible results quickly on the relevance and effectiveness of actions taken. Within this context, a focus on value for money, linking timely disaster spending to priorities and achievement of tangible outcomes, is no longer subject to negotiations. It is a given and part of the very fabric of a renewed interest and preoccupation with good governance.

RTE can be more complicated, and sometimes more resource intensive, than other evaluations, but it can provide a unique and opportune window on critical system level concerns, important indirect effects, and other disaster management issues. Above all, it provides a systematic, evidence-based analysis to counteract the hasty and erroneous perceptions that often emerge in emergency response.

References

Baker, J. (2005). Joint after-action review of our humanitarian response to the tsunami crisis. In *Proceedings of the CARE, Catholic Relief Services Workshop*, Bangkok, Thailand.

Beck, T. (2006). *Evaluating humanitarian action using the OECD-DAC criteria*. London: ALNAP.

Broughton, B., Maguire, S., Ahmed, H. Y., David-Toweh, K., Tonningen, L. R., Frueh, S., et al. (2006). *Inter-agency real-time evaluation of the humanitarian response to the Darfur crisis: A real-time evaluation commissioned by the United Nations Emergency Relief Coordinator and Under-Secretary-General for Humanitarian Affairs*. New York: Office for the Coordination of Humanitarian Affairs.

Cosgrave, J., Gonçalves, C., Martyris, D., Polastro, R., & Sikumba-Dils, M. (2007). *Inter-agency real-time evaluation of the response to the February 2007 floods and cyclone in Mozambique*. Geneva, Switzerland: Inter-Agency Standing Committee.

Cosgrave, J., Ramalingam, B., & Beck, T. (2009). *Real-time evaluations of humanitarian action: An ALNAP guide (pilot version)*. London: Active Learning Network for Accountability and Performance in Humanitarian Action.

Floret, N., Viel, J. F., Mauny, F., Hoen, B., & Piarroux, R. (2006). Negligible risk for epidemics after geophysical disasters. *Emerging Infectious Diseases, 14*, 543–548.

General Accounting Office, & Datta, L. (1990). *Prospective evaluation methods: The prospective evaluation synthesis* (Methodology Transfer Paper PEMD-10.1.10). Washington, DC: Program Evaluation and Methodology Division of the United States General Accounting Office. Retrieved July 4, 2009, from http://www.gao.gov/ special.pubs/pe10110.pdf

Hallam, A. (1998). *Evaluating humanitarian assistance programmes in complex emergencies* (RRN Good Practice Review 7). London: Overseas Development Institute.

Inter-Agency Standing Committee. (2006). *Real time evaluation: Application of the IASC cluster approach in the South Asia earthquake*. Islamabad, Pakistan: Author.

Krueger, R., & Casey, M. (2009). *Focus groups: A practical guide for applied research* (4th ed.). Thousand Oaks, CA: Sage.

Organisation for Economic Co-operation and Development, Development Assistance Committee. (1999). *Guidance for evaluating humanitarian assistance in complex emergencies 1999* (Evaluation and aid effectiveness 1). Paris: Author.

Organisation for Economic Co-operation and Development, Development Assistance Committee. (2002). *Glossary of key terms in evaluation and results based management*. Paris: Author.

Organisation for Economic Co-operation and Development, Development Assistance Committee. (2008). *Evaluating conflict prevention and peacebuilding activities: Working draft for application period*. A joint project of the DAC Network on Conflict, Peace and Development Co-operation and the DAC Network on Development Evaluation. Paris: Author.

Patton, M. (2002). *Qualitative research and evaluation methods*. Thousand Oaks, CA: Sage.

Sandison, P. (2003). *Desk review of real-time evaluation experience*. Manuscript in preparation. New York: UNICEF.

Scriven, M. (1991). *Evaluation thesaurus* (4th ed.). Newbury Park, CA: Sage.

Turner, R., Baker, J., Oo, Z. M., & Aye, N. S. (2008). *Inter-agency real time evaluation of the response to cyclone Nargis: 17 December 2008*. Geneva, Switzerland: Inter-Agency Standing Committee.

NEW DIRECTIONS FOR EVALUATION • DOI: 10.1002/ev

World Food Program Office. (2004). *Review of WFP's experience with real-time evaluation*. (Agenda item 2 for Executive Board Second Regular Session [WFP/EB.2/2004/2-B]). Rome, Italy: Author.

Yin, R. (2003). *Case study research: Design and methods* (3rd ed., Applied Social Research Methods Series: 5). Thousand Oaks, CA: Sage.

Young, N., Khattak, S. G., Bengali, K., & Elmi, L. (2007). *IASC inter-agency real-time evaluation of the Pakistan floods/Cyclone Yemyin: Final version*. New York: OCHA for the Inter-Agency Standing Committee.

EMERY BRUSSET is director of Channel Research, a research consultancy firm specializing in evaluations.

JOHN COSGRAVE is a professional evaluator and trainer in the humanitarian sector with InterWorks Europe.

WAYNE MACDONALD is director of Corporate Performance and Evaluation with Canada's Social Sciences and Humanities Research Council in Ottawa.

Bornemisza, O., Griekspoor, A., Ezard, N., & Sondorp, E. (2010). The Interagency Health and Nutrition Evaluation initiative in humanitarian crises: Moving from single-agency to joint, sectorwide evaluations. In L. A. Ritchie & W. MacDonald (Eds.), *Enhancing disaster and emergency preparedness, response, and recovery through evaluation*. New Directions for Evaluation, 126, 21–35

3

The Interagency Health and Nutrition Evaluation Initiative in Humanitarian Crises: Moving From Single-Agency to Joint, Sectorwide Evaluations

Olga Bornemisza, André Griekspoor, Nadine Ezard, Egbert Sondorp

Abstract

The authors focus on the growing international momentum for interagency or joint evaluations of humanitarian response. The Interagency Health and Nutrition Evaluation (IHE) initiative, established in 2003, is described and analyzed

The authors alone are responsible for the views expressed in this publication; these opinions do not necessarily represent the decisions, policies, or views of the World Health Organization.

The authors would like to thank various contributors who gave valuable input during the Interagency Health and Nutrition Evaluation (IHE) initiative. In particular, thanks are due to the many IHE working group members, including Ellen Girard-Barclay (consultant), Kate Burns (United Nations High Commission for Refugees [UNHCR]), Carmen Aramburu (UNHCR), Fathia Abdalla (UNHCR), Nadine Cornier (UNHCR), Susie Villeneuve (UNICEF), Peter Giesen (Médecins Sans Frontières-H), Elizabeth Berryman (Save the Children Fund UK), Linda Doull (Merlin), Oleg Bilhuka (CDC), Muireann Brennan (CDC), and members of the Bureau for Population, Refugees and Migration of the U.S. Department of State. Furthermore, we would like to thank everybody who took part in the implementation of the IHEs. Thanks are also due to BPRM, which funded the development of these guidelines.

NEW DIRECTIONS FOR EVALUATION, no. 126, Summer 2010 © Wiley Periodicals, Inc., and the American Evaluation Association. Published online in Wiley InterScience (www.interscience.wiley.com) • DOI: 10.1002/ev.327

in this chapter. The aims of IHE are described, as are the five components in the IHE framework of analysis: outcomes, service performance, policy and planning, risks to health and nutrition, and humanitarian context. This chapter focuses on lessons learned and identifies options for institutionalizing IHEs. © Wiley Periodicals, Inc., and the American Evaluation Association.

International humanitarian actors have not agreed on the best way to determine whether or not the health and nutrition needs of crisis-affected populations have been adequately met. In addition, attribution of achievement of specific humanitarian goals, such as reducing mortality and malnutrition, to specific humanitarian interventions remains difficult. Studies have demonstrated that international humanitarian responses are rarely triggered by, or are based on, objective estimates of needs of a population (Darcy & Hofmann, 2003). In response to these critiques, some progress has been made in the assessment of the health and nutrition needs of affected populations at the sector level, and at the level of the overall humanitarian system (Active Learning Network on Accountability and Performance [ALNAP], 2008a; Interagency Standing Committee [IASC] Consolidated Appeals Process [CAP] Sub–Working Group, 2006). For example, increased attention to needs assessment as a basis for setting priorities and determining effective interventions has been supported by several major bilateral donors. The Good Humanitarian Donorship (GHD) initiative created awareness of needs-based funding and advocated for more joint monitoring and evaluation, creating performance indicators to measure progress toward these goals (GHD, 2003). The Sphere project, launched in 1997 by a group of nongovernmental organizations (NGOs) and the Red Cross movement, published a handbook in 2004 on minimum standards for disaster response that covered several sectors, including health and nutrition. Discussion is still ongoing on how to use these standards for needs assessment and evaluation of humanitarian interventions. There has also been significant progress in the practice of evaluating humanitarian assistance. This was triggered by the Joint Evaluation of Emergency Assistance to Rwanda, which led to the creation of the ALNAP in 1997 (Borton, 1996).

Despite these developments, there is still no agreed-upon system for systematically monitoring and evaluating overall progress in meeting the health and nutrition needs of affected populations, and the performance of the international humanitarian assistance community towards that goal. Most evaluations of emergency response efforts since 1995 have been single-agency project evaluations. These have certain benefits in terms of being able to assess the effectiveness of a project and plausible impacts on a certain population. However, they also have limitations, including problems of attribution and the inability to examine how a specific project contributes to the broader humanitarian response. As no agency or donor has responsibility for the overall health and nutrition response in a particular crisis,

NEW DIRECTIONS FOR EVALUATION • DOI: 10.1002/ev

and none is accountable for the overall impact of their collective efforts, there is often little incentive to evaluate the collective response through joint evaluations.

Recently, however, there has been interest internationally in conducting more joint evaluations that have a broader scope (i.e., thematic, sectoral, multisectoral, or global) and that are interagency in nature (ALNAP, 2008a; Organization for Economic Cooperation and Development-Development Assistance Committee [OECD-DAC], 2006). For example, after the Indian Ocean tsunami in December 2004, the Tsunami Evaluation Coalition (TEC) conducted a systemwide, joint evaluation of the overall tsunami response, spurred by the enormous loss of life and subsequent attention this disaster received. Interest in conducting more joint evaluations is due to recognition that broader evaluations need to be done to examine the overall coverage, effectiveness, and appropriateness of a specific humanitarian response. In addition, only joint, sectorwide evaluations can analyze performance of service delivery from the perspective of the entire affected population rather than from the perspective of individual humanitarian agencies, which tend to target their activities (ALNAP, 2008a). Joint evaluations will not replace the need for single-agency project evaluations, as each agency remains accountable to those who fund them, and these evaluations are important for internal learning and improvement of program performance. However, if higher level, contextual issues were adequately addressed in joint evaluations, these would not have to be covered by single-agency evaluations, which would simplify the latter.

Within this context, the Interagency Health and Nutrition (IHE) initiative was established by a group of United Nations (UN) agencies, NGOs, donors, and institutions involved in humanitarian disaster assistance, spearheaded by the World Health Organization (WHO) and United Nations High Commissioner for Refugees (UNHCR).

The Core Working Group consisted of Action Contre la Faim-France/ Action Against Hunger–UK, the Centers for Disease Control and Prevention (CDC), Epicentre, the London School of Hygiene and Tropical Medicine (LSHTM), Merlin, MSF-Holland, Save the Children UK, United Nations Population Fund (UNFPA), UNHCR, United Nations Children's Fund (UNICEF), United Nations World Food Program (WFP), and WHO.

The aim of the IHE initiative was to assess international performance in the health and nutrition sector during the emergency response and recovery phase. It also aimed to complement single-agency evaluations by exploring how agencies collaborate and how they address wider policy issues within a humanitarian setting. This chapter describes the rationale for the IHE initiative, the evaluation process and lessons learned, and ongoing challenges to conducting and mainstreaming interagency, sectorwide evaluations in the health and nutrition sector.

Rationale for the IHE Initiative

The agencies involved in the IHE initiative felt it was important to evaluate the overall effectiveness of humanitarian health and nutrition interventions, as these can make an essential contribution to the reduction of avoidable morbidity and mortality. Evidence indicates that in the majority of international humanitarian crises, deaths are due to preventable communicable diseases and malnutrition, not violence (Coghlan et al., 2006; Salama, Spiegel, Talley, & Waldman, 2004). However, evaluating health care and nutrition services is particularly complex, as myriad agencies are involved, including several UN agencies, national and international NGOs, national health authorities, and donor agencies. All have varying legal mandates, policy interests, time frames, target populations, resource capacities, activities, and exit strategies. Moreover, health and nutrition responses vary from time-limited, targeted life-saving interventions, such as control of an outbreak, to (re)establishing comprehensive preventive and curative nutrition and health services based on primary health care principles (Sphere Project, 2004). Other factors, such as working in dynamic situations with fluctuating insecurity and population movements, affect implementation, whereby earlier achievements may be lost entirely. It is therefore not surprising that no consensual programming framework exists. Humanitarian health and nutrition responses should be context specific and adaptive over time, depending on burden of disease trends, and the health actors and resources available. Decisions are based as much on judgment as on data, and are highly influenced by politics and resource availability (Roberts, 2007; von Schreeb, Unge, Brittain-Long, & Rosling, 2008). The evaluation of such dynamic, context-specific responses is therefore complex.

In addition, health and nutrition services cannot be evaluated without taking national health systems and local capacities into account. National health systems are usually disrupted because of the conflict; problems can include a severe lack of qualified health workers, fragmented drug supply systems, and looted infrastructure and financing systems that may impose barriers to access, or lead to catastrophic expenditures. Health and nutrition information systems are usually dysfunctional, and often do not allow for aggregation of data between various stakeholders. These complex health system issues cannot be analyzed from a single-agency perspective, which is why joint, sectorwide evaluations complement single-agency evaluations.

Accepted standards against which to evaluate the overall health and nutrition sector do not exist (Bradt & Drummond, 2003; Spiegel, Burkle, Dev, & Salama, 2001). There is no agreed-upon process that involves all relevant stakeholders (including affected populations), no agreed-upon logical framework with sectorwide objectives, no commonly agreed-upon indicators that can be used to monitor overall progress in performance, no established monitoring protocols, and no reliable data collection systems. The closest humanitarian agencies come to outlining sector-specific, minimum standards for health and nutrition services are those formulated in the Sphere Handbook (Sphere Project, 2004), as well as in some UN Interagency Standing Committee (IASC) Common Humanitarian Action Plans (CHAP). However, the Sphere Handbook is not meant to be a logical framework, and only a minority of the Sphere standards are quantifiable and evidence-based (Roberts & Helderman, 2008). The CHAP is still mainly used as a fund-raising tool for selected agencies, and not (yet) as a programming tool for all humanitarian stakeholders. Proposals to establish a performance-monitoring system for health and nutrition have made slow progress (Griekspoor, Loretti, & Colombo, 2005). The Standardized Monitoring and Assessment of Relief and Transitions (SMART) initiative (n.d.) has done work on needs assessment and monitoring, as has the Health and Nutrition Tracking Service (HNTS) established by the IASC Health and Nutrition Clusters in 2005 (World Health Organization [WHO], 2008b). Emphasis has been on mortality and malnutrition rates as indicators of trends and overall impact on survival. Knowing these rates at the population level is extremely important, as they indicate the urgency of the situation (Checchi, Gayer, Grais, & Mills, 2007), but they are not so useful in assessing how international humanitarian health and nutrition relief efforts need to improve. To address these challenges, and to stimulate the use of joint evaluation in the health and nutrition sector, the IHE initiative was created in 2003.

The IHE Process

The IHE initiative conducted six joint health and nutrition evaluations between 2003 and 2006. They were formative evaluations, "intended to improve performance, most often conducted during the implementation phase of projects or programs" (OECD-DAC, 2002). They were also interagency in that all the health and nutrition agencies (UN, NGO, donor, national health authorities) that worked in a specific humanitarian context were invited to participate. Each evaluation cost about $50,000–70,000, excluding management costs of the various IHE partners in their headquarters and costs incurred by the agencies that supported the missions on the ground. Key elements of the IHE evaluations are presented in Table 3.1.

The first three pilot evaluations conducted in the autumn of 2003 examined the health and nutrition situation of refugees in Nepal, Zambia, and Pakistan. To reflect on the experience of these pilot evaluations, and to discuss the way forward, a background paper was commissioned (Poletti, 2004), and a conference was held in March 2004 (Interagency Health and Nutrition Evaluation Initiative, 2004). A core working group (CWG) was formed to provide oversight to the initiative (Action Contre le Faim France/Action Against Hunger UK, CDC USA, Epicentre, LSHTM, International Federation of the Red Cross, Merlin, MSF-Holland, Save the Children UK, UNHCR, UNICEF, WFP, and WHO), and an additional 25 agencies agreed

Table 3.1. Key Elements of Interagency Health and Nutrition Evaluations (IHEs)

Evaluation of collective action	IHEs evaluate collective performance of health and nutrition programming in a specific geographic area where a humanitarian crisis is occurring, from the perspective of the affected population and seeking the opinion of said population.
Interagency in nature	IHEs are interagency evaluations in which all health and nutrition agencies (UN, NGO, donor, national health authorities) that work in a specific geographic area take part. A local IHE steering committee manages the process, sometimes with external assistance.
Lesson learning and accountability	IHEs can be done in real time to inform ongoing activities so that action can be taken to improve the response. They can also be done to encourage broader lesson learning and accountability in the humanitarian system.
Common framework and indicators	IHEs use a common evaluative framework (Figure 3.1) that details the topics for evaluation, as well as performance indicators for the health and nutrition sector.
Action planning	Agency managers formulate a point-by-point management response to the recommendations and/or main findings of the IHE.

to form a larger, consultative IHE Stakeholders Group to oversee the process. A part-time project coordinator was hired to manage the evaluations. Between April 2004 and December 2006, the CWG organized three more evaluations in Burundi, Liberia, and Chad. Follow-up missions and planning workshops were conducted in Chad and Liberia in November and December 2006. Each was conducted by a team of two to three health and nutrition experts over a period of 3–4 weeks. Based on these experiences, IHE guidelines were developed (Interagency Health and Nutrition Evaluation Initiative, 2007) that include an evaluative framework. See Figure 3.1.

The framework includes five key areas that an IHE should take into account:

1. Health and nutrition outcomes, such as mortality and malnutrition rates.
2. Performance of health and nutrition services, including provision (availability, accessibility, and quality), utilization and coverage of services.
3. Health and nutrition sector policy and strategic planning, including leadership, health information systems, medical products and technologies, health workforce; health financing and humanitarian funding

Figure 3.1. IHE Evaluation Framework

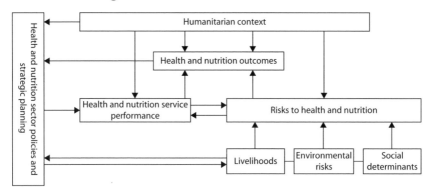

are cross-cutting health system issues that influence the delivery of, and/or access to, adequate services.

4. Risks to health and nutrition, such as environmental risks related to water and sanitation, food security, forced migration, the potential for outbreaks of communicable diseases, and risk of natural hazards.

5. The humanitarian context, such as the security and human rights situation of the affected population, protection issues, and the humanitarian space.

Primary users were decision makers at the country level, including heads of mission and health coordinators of NGOs, policy makers within the Ministries of Health and their counterparts in the UN system, and donors with country-level presence. To optimize the utility of the IHEs, the purpose, objectives, and methods of each evaluation were adapted to the specific context. For example, IHEs conducted in refugee settings evaluated health service provision for displaced populations and the dynamic relationship with locally available health services. In postconflict settings such as Liberia, health service delivery was analyzed with regards to plans for health system reconstruction, repatriation of refugees, and return of internally displaced populations.

Lessons Learned

A review of the six evaluations suggests that IHEs showed promise in a number of areas that cannot be addressed by single-agency efforts. These areas, similar to those of other international joint evaluations (ALNAP, 2008b), were related to the interagency process, broad policy focus, and attention to how the results would be used.

Interagency Process. The IHEs promoted collaboration and trust between agencies, and engaged national health authorities in the evaluation process. Midway through the process, it became apparent that field-level ownership and use of the IHEs needed to be strengthened. To achieve this, previsits by an external evaluator were added to the IHE process in Burundi and Liberia. These were then also used to maximize engagement of multiple actors through the local exiting coordination mechanisms, similar to real time evaluations (Cosgrave, Ramalingam, & Beck, 2009). Local steering committees were established, consisting of key humanitarian actors in the health sector and Ministry of Health staff. The steering committees provided valuable input into the terms of reference drafted by the CWG and managed the implementation of the IHE. These committees also arranged debriefing sessions at the end of the evaluation, during which joint action planning was conducted in order to implement the recommendations. In Chad, competing priorities of humanitarian actors and volatile security precluded a previsit, limiting buy-in and utilization of the evaluation by other agencies, and shifting the burden of organizing the evaluation onto one agency, thereby demonstrating the importance of the previsit.

Strengthening Coordination, Policy, and Planning. IHEs made an important contribution to the policy process in the transition from emergency to postemergency response. For example, the Liberian IHE identified important shortfalls when shifting from humanitarian to development funding, and this analysis was instrumental in subsequent policy and funding decisions (Vergeer, Canavan, & Bornemisza, 2008). IHEs also gave relevant recommendations and identified gaps in higher-level coordination approaches, strategic planning, and policy frameworks, such as the relationship between humanitarian and local health service provision.

Using the Results. All evaluation and follow-up reports were sent to key stakeholders, and were placed on the Internet to enhance accessibility. As the IHEs were intended to produce useful results and be action oriented, follow-up visits by the evaluators were incorporated into the evaluation process. In the two countries where they were conducted, Liberia and Chad, they aimed to embed the evaluation process in the field, to assess whether progress had been made on the recommendations, and to provoke further discussion and action planning. Although these objectives were met, after the follow-up evaluations were completed it was not possible to track to what extent subsequent recommendations were formally incorporated into ongoing management responses by the various agencies involved. This is partly linked to the fact that at health-sector level, there is no single stakeholder with the responsibility for management follow-up.

Challenges

Several challenges remain to be addressed before IHEs can be mainstreamed into humanitarian action. These can be divided into technical and governance issues.

NEW DIRECTIONS FOR EVALUATION • DOI: 10.1002/ev

Technical Dilemmas. The technical issues that remain to be addressed are as follows.

Defining the Scope of IHEs. A continuing challenge in designing IHEs was defining the scope of the evaluation. In the six pilots, the focus of the evaluation was context specific and varied from mainly programmatic to higher-level policy, or a mix of both. This variation was related to the differences in contexts, as well as by the different expectations and demands from the national stakeholders.

It was recognized that interagency approaches cannot be everything to everybody, and that choices must be made given time and resource restrictions. Terms of reference for multi-stakeholder evaluations can be overambitious, which can lead to disappointment when expectations are not fully met. Managing these diverse requirements and expectations will require negotiating clear expected outputs, resource flows, and accountability frameworks; using an agreed-upon evaluation framework may help with aligning expectations. Flexibility in defining the scope of each evaluation is essential, and more work on guiding this decision-making process is necessary.

Standardization of Evaluation Methods. Evaluation methods varied, but among the approaches used were literature reviews, secondary quantitative data synthesis and analysis, primary quantitative data collection, key informant interviews, and focus groups or group interviews with service providers and primary stakeholders, including beneficiaries. Epidemiological surveys were not done as they were difficult to implement in the short time periods available. Instead, IHEs assessed whether appropriate surveys and resulting epidemiological data were available, and if the results were used to inform policy.

The choice of methods used depended on the objectives of a specific IHE and available evidence. Typically, readily available, robust, and comparable epidemiological and funding data to enable comparison of needs, response effectiveness, and funding allocation across crises were unavailable. Nevertheless, within the CWG there was a tension between a desire to standardize evaluation methodologies based on quantitative, indicator-based methods to allow direct comparison between countries, versus context-specific, more qualitative policy-based approaches that focus on flexibility and responsiveness to the needs of the field. It was agreed that some degree of comparability of information was desirable at a systemwide level, but that IHEs are not summative impact studies, which require rigorous epidemiological approaches (Network of Networks on Impact Evaluations [NONIE], 2009). Instead, IHEs examined the available evidence to support judgments on impact. In the future, we believe that IHEs should be seen as complementary to ongoing initiatives such as SMART and the HNTS that aim to improve and standardize the availability of quantitative data at outcome and impact levels from humanitarian settings.

Including Affected Populations. Evaluation of humanitarian assistance is not complete without involving the affected population (Grunewald & de Geoffrey, 2008). The commitment to be more accountable to affected populations is reflected by, for example, the Code of Conduct for the International Red Cross Movement and NGOs in Disaster Relief (http://www.ifrc.org/publicat/conduct/code.asp), the Humanitarian Accountability Partnership (HAP) (http://www.hapinternational.org/), and the Sphere Humanitarian Charter (http://www.sphereproject.org/), which all advocate for a rights-based approach to humanitarian aid. As such, sectorwide evaluations should make dedicated efforts to solicit the views of affected populations. The six evaluations varied in the degree to which such population views were included in the IHE. Crisis-affected people were interviewed, or participated in focus groups in all of the IHEs, but none went further to ensure their engagement in planning, implementation, or follow-up. There is a growing emphasis on participatory processes in humanitarian health response (ALNAP, 2003; United Nations High Commission for Refugees [UNHCR], 2006), and more work is required to improve community engagement in the IHE process.

Availability of Trained and Skilled Evaluators. There were a lack of trained international and national evaluators with the right mix of public health, humanitarian, and evaluation insights, and skilled at the sectorwide level, a finding already noted by others (ALNAP, 2008b). However, the IHE demonstrated that evaluators who have excellent project-level evaluation experience could conduct good sectorwide evaluations if they were given well-written terms of reference, were diligently briefed, and were on a team with complementary skills and experience. Efforts were also made to create teams of mixed gender, and to include both national and international evaluators. Nevertheless, more investment is required in training evaluators, both at the international and national levels, in sectorwide and interagency approaches to evaluation.

Governance Issues. The governance issues that remain to be addressed are as follows.

Timing of the Evaluation and Linkages With the Strategic Planning Cycle. All IHEs were conducted in chronic situations, more than 3 years after the onset of the political crisis. The timing of the IHE within the phase of a crisis influenced its terms of reference; for example, they were used to guide the recovery process or to analyze the adequacy of preparedness.

To ensure that the findings of the evaluation were used by humanitarian actors, it was important to identify key decision-making processes, such as a new Consolidated Appeal Process (CAP) planning cycle. Experience showed that this was difficult to achieve, and that more effort was needed to better integrate them into the formal IASC continuum of assessment, planning, monitoring, and evaluation. If the IASC needs-analysis framework (NAF) and the CAP/CHAP processes were used as a baseline for monitoring or evaluation, IHEs could be linked to these processes; for instance, they could be formally included toward the end of a CAP cycle.

Based on our experience, IHEs should be conducted within 3–6 months of a new acute major international crisis and/or after 12–24 months in a chronic situation. Other factors that may influence the timing of an IHE include the implementation of other evaluations, such as real-time evaluations. Other triggers for an IHE could be a substantial change in the humanitarian context (i.e., a renewed outbreak of the conflict or a new transitional peace process) or the humanitarian response (e.g., decreased funding flows). They may also help when a situation has stagnated in terms of the humanitarian context and/or the humanitarian response (e.g., neglected emergencies).

Commissioning of IHEs. The nature of the humanitarian aid and the diffusion of responsibilities for action are a barrier to routine implementation of joint evaluations. No single agency has responsibility for the overall health and nutrition response in a particular humanitarian crisis. As such, none has the responsibility to commission sectorwide evaluations. Individual donors finance only certain NGO or UN agencies to deliver care to parts of the crisis-affected population, and are not held individually accountable for the overall impact of their collective investments. Attempts are underway to call for more joint evaluation, for instance, via the GHD initiative. Progress is unclear, although eight joint evaluations were reported in a recent GHD progress report (Development Initiatives, 2008).

Within the UN, there is no clear responsibility for overall response in the health and nutrition sector. Since the creation of the UN Office for the Coordination of Humanitarian Affairs (OCHA) and the CAPs, UN agencies are expected to take responsibility for joint planning and filling gaps, but this responsibility exists mostly *de jure*, not *de facto*. Humanitarian reforms in 2005 led to the creation of the cluster approach, whereby for each emergency, agencies coordinate under one umbrella, with a lead agency. Global clusters are supposed to support national clusters. The cluster approach aims to ensure better accountability and predictability, in part by clarifying roles and responsibilities (Interagency Standing Committee, 2009). WHO is the global cluster lead agency for health, and UNICEF is the lead agency for nutrition. Despite these reforms, funding remains fragmented, with different agencies receiving funding from different donors. Cluster leads are not always able to fill the role of last provider due to lack of resources and capacity, and the overwhelming scale of the global response needed (Graves, Wheeler, & Martin, 2007; WHO, 2008a). Also, stakeholders in the clusters are not formally accountable to the lead agency, but are responsible to their funder in terms of reporting on progress.

Assigning Responsibility for Follow-Up. The follow-up of recommendations remains challenging, and is compounded by unclear responsibilities among different stakeholders, and lack of institutionalization for joint, sector-specific evaluations. The IHE initiative arranged follow-up missions to document changes since the previous evaluation, and to follow up on particular recommendations for specific agencies. However, there were a number of barriers to follow-up for both the IHE initiative and for the agencies involved. Fragmented planning, prioritization, and funding processes made it difficult to ensure the IHE evaluators were in country when relevant planning meetings were taking place. High staff turnover within agencies resulted in the disbanding of several steering committees, and precluded a follow-up mission in Burundi, for example. For agencies, acting upon evaluative recommendations was voluntary; the IHE initiative and the local steering committee had no power beyond peer review and persuasion, which may have limited the effectiveness of the IHEs and their accountability. Despite these difficulties, there was a sense from the evaluators that recommendations that could be easily addressed by agencies were often implemented, and that the evaluations led to useful discussions about how to overcome some of the more difficult, often structural problems in the health and nutrition sector.

Making findings available to those higher up in the system, such as headquarters staff and donor representatives, remained difficult. In most cases, in-country staff and local steering committee members forwarded reports to their headquarters and donors, but it was difficult to ensure that this was done systematically. Follow-up also implied organizational learning, and required changes to internal and interagency processes. Although evaluations can stimulate this, they are often not a sufficient driver of change (ALNAP, 2006).

Future Directions: Institutionalizing IHEs

The diffuse international responsibility and fragmented funding for the health and nutrition sector means that it is difficult to assign responsibilities to commission and follow-up on IHEs. However, as they are potentially an important tool for improving the overall humanitarian response, efforts should be made to embed them into the institutional structure of the international humanitarian system.

The most logical setting for institutionalizing joint, sectorwide evaluations is via the existing in-country IASC health or nutrition clusters, supported by the global health and nutrition clusters. The IASC Global Health Cluster core commitments include the responsibility to "develop common methodologies for conducting joint evaluations and gathering lessons learned" (IASC Global Health Cluster, 2008). As such, these clusters are best placed to initiate, manage, and fund interagency health and nutrition evaluations. The clusters would be able to provide technical support from their large pool of technical staff, and allocate resources and a small team of people to manage them. Placing IHEs within the clusters would help institutionalize them; as a recent review of joint evaluations found, evaluations benefited from being part of established institutional arrangements, as this enabled them to tap into established mechanisms for engagement and follow-up (ALNAP, 2008b).

If and when they are institutionalized, and more IHEs are conducted, donors and other key decision makers should collate common findings across evaluation reports, synthesizing and illuminating common trends, problems, and lessons learned. IHEs could thus function as summative evaluations by encouraging broader lesson learning in the international humanitarian system. Although the focus of IHEs should be to improve learning and performance, they could also function as a form of collective accountability, reflecting the combined response of key stakeholders.

Conclusion

Interagency health and nutrition evaluations can make valuable contributions to the performance of international humanitarian assistance. As sectorwide evaluations, IHEs fill a niche in the spectrum of evaluation practices, adding value at a level that single-agency evaluations cannot address. At the same time, IHEs pose new challenges that are not yet fully resolved, partly reflecting underlying structural weaknesses in the humanitarian system. They cannot respond to everyone's needs. Each group of stakeholders has different information needs, and requirements for accountability and learning. These range from policy-oriented to operational type analyses, with different levels of detail required. As a result, no single evaluation can cover all issues, and prioritization is necessary. In addition, there is no single stakeholder in the health and nutrition sector with overall responsibility for the policy process, implementation, and control over resources. The IASC Health and Nutrition Clusters come closest, and as such, they are well placed to commission and manage further IHEs.

In order to mainstream interagency health and nutrition evaluations into the humanitarian sector, two things need to occur. First, more work is required on the technical side: developing an analytical framework and approaches for defining the scope of work; choosing a mix of methodologies that ensures a balance between standardization for comparability versus context-specific analyses; and ways to include the views of affected people into IHEs. Second, in terms of governance, there is a need to institutionalize health and nutrition sectorwide evaluations. Clear and inclusive leadership is needed to designate responsibilities for the commissioning, funding, use, and follow-up. Integrating them in the clusters would ensure that they are given the appropriate technical and managerial support. More interagency evaluations of this type will help to improve the effectiveness of the health and nutrition sector and ultimately benefit those who receive humanitarian aid.

References

Active Learning Network on Accountability and Performance. (2003). *Participation by crisis-affected populations in humanitarian action: A handbook for practitioners.* London: ODI.
Active Learning Network on Accountability and Performance. (2006). The utilisation of evaluations. In J. Mitchell (Ed.), *ALNAP review of humanitarian action, evaluation utilization* (Chapter 3). London: ODI.

Active Learning Network on Accountability and Performance. (2008a). *Annual review of humanitarian action.* London: ODI.

Active Learning Network on Accountability and Performance. (2008b). Joint evaluation coming of age? The quality and future scope of future evaluations. In M. Herson, J. Mitchell, & B. Ramalingam (Eds.), *ALNAP seventh review of humanitarian action* (Chapter 3). London: ODI.

Borton, J. (1996, June). The joint evaluation of emergency assistance to Rwanda. *Humanitarian Exchange, 5.*

Bradt, D., & Drummond, C. 2003. Rapid epidemiological assessment of health status in displaced populations: An evolution toward standardized minimum, essential data sets. *Prehospital Disaster Medicine, 18,* 178–185.

Checchi, F., Gayer, M., Grais, R., & Mills, E. (2007). *Public health in crisis affected populations: A practical guide for decision makers.* London: ODI.

Coghlan, B., Brennan, R., Ngoy, P., Dafara, D., Otto, B., Clements, M., et al. (2006). Mortality in the Democratic Republic of Congo: A nationwide survey. *Lancet, 367,* 44–51.

Cosgrave, J., Ramalingam, B., & Beck, T. (2009). *Real-time evaluations of humanitarian action: An ALNAP guide, pilot version.* London: ODI.

Darcy, J., & Hofmann, C. A. (2003). *According to need? Needs assessment and decision-making in the humanitarian sector* (HPG Report 15). London: ODI Humanitarian Policy Group (HPG).

Development Initiatives. (2008). *Good humanitarian donorship (GHD) indicators report.* (GHD Report). Stockholm, Sweden: Good Humanitarian Donorship Initiative.

Good Humanitarian Donorship Initiative. (2003). Principles and good practice of humanitarian donorship. In *Good humanitarian donorship initiative.* Stockholm, Sweden: Author. Retrieved from http://www.reliefweb.int/ghd/a%2023%20Principles%20EN-GHD19.10.04%20RED.doc

Graves, S., Wheeler, V., & Martin, E. (2007). *Lost in translation: Managing coordination and leadership reform in the humanitarian system* (HPG Policy Brief 27). London: ODI Humanitarian Policy Group.

Griekspoor, A., Loretti, A., & Colombo, A. (2005). *Tracking the performance of essential health and nutrition services in humanitarian responses.* Background paper prepared for the WHO Workshop on Tracking Health Performance and Humanitarian Outcomes. Geneva, Switzerland: WHO.

Grunewald, F., & de Geoffrey, V. (2008). *Request implementing humanitarian organisations to ensure to the greatest possible extent, adequate involvement of beneficiaries in the design, implementation, monitoring and evaluation of humanitarian response.* (Principle 7 Policy Paper). Groupe URD, Commissioned by the Humanitarian Aid Delegation of the French Ministry for Foreign and European Affairs. Retrieved from http://www.goodhumanitariandonorship.org/documents/080930_ghdi_principle_7_final.doc

Interagency Health and Nutrition Evaluation (IHE) Initiative. (2004, March). *Proceedings of the Inter-Agency Health Evaluations in Crises Workshop,* Geneva, Switzerland. London: Author.

Interagency Health and Nutrition Evaluation (IHE) Initiative. (2007). *Guidelines for implementing interagency health and nutrition evaluations in humanitarian crises.* London: Author.

Interagency Standing Committee. (2009). *Cluster approach and humanitarian reform.* Retrieved June 29, 2009, from http://www.humanitarianreform.org/humanitarianreform/Default.aspx?tabid=70

Interagency Standing Committee Consolidated Appeal Process Sub–working Group. (2006). *The needs analysis framework: Strengthening the process of analysis and presentation of humanitarian needs in the CAP.* Geneva, Switzerland: Author.

Interagency Standing Committee Global Health Cluster. (2008). *IASC Global Health Cluster mission statement and core commitments.* Geneva, Switzerland: Author.

Network of Networks on Impact Evaluations. (2009). *Draft guidance on impact evaluation.*

OECD-DAC. (2002). *Glossary of key terms in evaluation and results based management.* OECD-DAC Working Party on Aid Evaluation Report 6. Retrieved from http://www.oecd.org/dataoecd/29/21/2754804.pdf

OECD-DAC. (2006). *Guidance for managing joint evaluations.* DAC Evaluation Series. Paris: Author.

Poletti, T. (2004). *Inter-agency health evaluations in humanitarian crises: A background issues paper.* London: London School of Hygiene and Tropical Medicine, Conflict and Health Programme.

Roberts, L. (2007). Advances in monitoring have not translated into improvements in humanitarian health services. *Prehospital and Disaster Medicine, 22,* 384–389.

Roberts, L., & Helderman, T. (2008). *Priority indicators in complex emergencies: Summary of a consultancy for the health and nutrition tracking system.* Geneva, Switzerland: WHO.

Salama, P., Spiegel, P., Talley, L., & Waldman, R. (2004). Lessons learned from complex emergencies over past decade. *Lancet, 364,* 801–813.

SMART Initiative. (n.d.) Retrieved June 29, 2009, from http://www.smartindicators.org/

Sphere Project. (2004). *Humanitarian charter and minimum standards in disaster response.* Geneva, Switzerland: Author.

Spiegel, P. B., Burkle, F. M., Dev, C. C., & Salama, P. (2001). Developing public health indicators in complex emergency response. *Prehospital Disaster Medicine, 16,* 281–285.

United Nations High Commission for Refugees. (2006). *The UNHCR tool for participatory assessment in operations.* Geneva, Switzerland: Author.

Vergeer, P., Canavan, A., & Bornemisza, O. (2008). *Post-conflict health sectors: The myth and reality of post-conflict funding gaps.* London: Health and Fragile States Network.

von Schreeb, J., Unge, C., Brittain-Long, R., & Rosling, H. (2008). Are donor allocations for humanitarian health assistance based on needs assessment data? *Global Public Health 3,* 1–8.

World Health Organization. (2008a). *Global health cluster.* Geneva, Switzerland: Author.

World Health Organization. (2008b). *Health action in crises: Primary health care in crises* (WHO Annual Report). Geneva, Switzerland: Author.

OLGA BORNEMISZA *is a research fellow with the Conflict and Health Program in the Health Policy Unit at the London School of Hygiene and Tropical Medicine.*

ANDRÉ GRIEKSPOOR *is senior evaluation adviser in the Evaluation and Performance Audit unit at the World Health Organization in Geneva.*

NADINE EZARD *is a senior research fellow with the Monash Initiative for Global Health Improvement, Monash University, and formerly senior public health officer at UNHCR at the time the work was conducted.*

EGBERT SONDORP *is a senior lecturer with the Conflict and Health Program in the Health Policy Unit of the London School of Hygiene and Tropical Medicine.*

Steinke-Chase, M., & Tranzillo, D. (2010). Save the Children's approach to emergency evaluation and learning: Evolution in policy and practice. In L. A. Ritchie & W. MacDonald (Eds.), *Enhancing disaster and emergency preparedness, response, and recovery through evaluation. New Directions for Evaluation, 126,* 37–49.

4

Save the Children's Approach to Emergency Evaluation and Learning: Evolution in Policy and Practice

Megan Steinke-Chase, Danielle Tranzillo

Abstract

The humanitarian assistance sector has developed globally from a state of spontaneous and disjointed approaches, and is striving to be more deliberate, coordinated, and accountable. Save the Children's experience has paralleled that evolution. This chapter explores advances in emergency evaluation approaches, utilization, and learning that have driven systematic improvements in Save the Children's policy and practice as it responds to major emergencies. It discusses challenges and successful efforts to internalize sector standards, ensure participation of affected populations, strengthen coordination across the sector, and increase impact measurement of emergency response. © Wiley Periodicals, Inc., and the American Evaluation Association.

The 2004 publication, *Ambiguity and Change: Humanitarian NGOs Prepare for the Future,* by the Feinstein International Famine Center at Tufts University, depicted nongovernmental organizations (NGOs) at a point of unprecedented influence, credibility, and responsibility. As a major socioeconomic force, the nonprofit sector faces new and changing demands from internal and external stakeholders for legitimacy, accountability, and transparency. To meet these demands, and ensure accountability to all stakeholders, Save the Children has committed to strengthening its approaches to evaluation and coordination in all emergency responses, both in the United States and internationally.

Since the late 1980s, the humanitarian sector has approached evaluation and learning in more deliberate, coordinated, and measurable ways. The development of emergency evaluation approaches and the utilization of learning are driving systematic improvements not only in the humanitarian assistance sector, but also in Save the Children's own emergency response policy and practice. This chapter looks at the critical shifts in emergency evaluation and learning at Save the Children. It brings together the results of a review of external publications; internal and external evaluations of emergency responses, policies, and other learning documentation; key informant interviews with Save the Children staff; and the authors' observations as employees of Save the Children from 1995 to 2009.

Origins and Impetus

International disaster response has changed dramatically over the past 50 years, driven by analysis and learning from previous humanitarian responses to make systematic improvements.

The first international humanitarian laws binding state and nonstate actors to standards ensuring the protection of civilians in armed conflict culminated in 1949 with the Third and Fourth Geneva Conventions. From this moment, humanitarian sectorwide initiatives were launched to improve the transparency, accountability, and quality of emergency response and to uphold the commitment to deliver on a humanitarian imperative "to provide humanitarian assistance wherever it is needed," as defined by the *Code of Conduct for The International Red Cross and Red Crescent Movement and NGOs in Disaster Relief* (2004).

In 1962, the International Council of Voluntary Agencies (ICVA) formed as an advocacy alliance for humanitarian action. The ICVA works as a collective body to promote and advocate for human rights and a humanitarian perspective in global debates and responses. The Steering Committee for Humanitarian Response (SCHR), formed in 1972, brings together international humanitarian actors, including Save the Children, to share information, foster cooperation, and develop common positions and practices where possible.

Compelled by the frequency and scale of international emergencies in the 1970s and 1980s, such as the Cambodian refugee crisis, the Ethiopian drought, the conflict in Somalia, and the escalating crisis in the Balkans, the United Nations (UN) Department of Humanitarian Affairs (today the Office for Coordination of Humanitarian Affairs [OCHA]), was formed in 1991 to promote coherence and to coordinate response activities among UN agencies and their partners. In 1994, the SCHR members adopted the *Code of Conduct for The International Red Cross and Red Crescent Movement and*

NGOs in Disaster Relief (2004) to articulate standards of effectiveness and impact in disaster response.

In response to the 1996 multiagency evaluation, "The International Response to Conflict and Genocide: Lessons from the Rwanda Experience" (Steering Committee of the Joint Evaluation of Emergency Assistance to Rwanda, 1996), independent agencies developed standards and norms for various aspects of emergency response. These included The Sphere Project, Active Learning Network for Accountability and Performance in Humanitarian Action (ALNAP), Inter-Agency Network for Education in Emergencies, and the Humanitarian Accountability Partnership (HAP). These were important initiatives, all of which Save the Children helped shape. Coalitions were also formed to improve emergency response. Examples of these coalitions are the Inter-Agency Standing Committee, Emergency Capacity Building Project (ECB), and more recently, the Tsunami Evaluation Coalition (TEC; 2006) and Clinton NGO Impact Initiative.

During this time coordination across the International Save the Children Alliance, a federation of 29 international member organizations, also increased. In 1996, Save the Children established an emergency liaison team to improve coordination of emergency responses across its member organizations. This central coordinating body remains today.

In March 2003, seven agencies (CARE International, Catholic Relief Services, International Rescue Committee, Mercy Corps, Oxfam [UK], SC, and World Vision International) convened to discuss the most persistent obstacles in humanitarian aid delivery and commissioned an analysis of each organization's emergency response capacity. The 2004 *Report on Emergency Capacity* (Braun, 2004) highlighted accountability and impact measurement as areas needing additional capacity within and across all organizations. The report also served as the catalyst for launching the Gates Foundation–funded Emergency Capacity Building project (ECB) to ensure agency commitments translated into practice.

Monitoring and Evaluation Policies and Resources at Save the Children

During responses to the Iraq conflict and the Darfur crisis in the early 2000s, Save the Children had limited capacity to establish monitoring systems at the outset of each response. This challenged the agency's ability to evaluate performance. One central staff position was charged with overseeing monitoring and evaluation for development *and* emergency programs; not surprisingly this position experienced periods of turnover and vacancy.

The Southeast Asia tsunami (hereafter referred to as tsunami), Hurricane Katrina, and the 2005 earthquake in northwest Pakistan and Kashmir (hereafter referred to as Batagram Earthquake) marked a turning point. Conducting three major emergency responses at more or less the same time while also responding to smaller- and medium-scale disasters severely taxed the organization's staffing and systems. The international tsunami response and Hurricane Katrina response in the United States created an unprecedented demand for accountability. Although Save the Children completed assessments to inform program design and evaluated all three responses, the agency still lacked monitoring and evaluation staff, strong data management, and monitoring tools on the ground. This made introducing performance management tools more difficult once programs were under way.

Given the frequency and scale of emergencies in 2005, Save the Children established a staff position focused on stakeholder accountability and agency performance, in the context of the interagency and systemwide response to the tsunami. Additionally, the organization created a full-time emergency assessment, design, monitoring, and evaluation (ADME) position to lead the development and rollout of a comprehensive ADME system for Save the Children's emergency programming in headquarters and the field. Learning from the ECB project moved accountability and impact measurement from a grant focus to an agency priority. Related objectives appeared centrally in Save the Children's 2005–2007 and 2008–2012 agency strategic plans, and translated into changes in organizational policy and practice.

Save the Children's monitoring and evaluation of responses to Cyclones Sidr in Bangladesh (2007) and Nargis in Myanmar (2008) was improved based on earlier learning. For example, program and monitoring and evaluation staff worked together from assessments through implementation and final evaluation; staff shared evaluations with the larger humanitarian community through the ALNAP website. Reviews and evaluations included case studies that provided a more in-depth look at children's feedback on the response, engagement of civil society actors, work with village committees, and adherence to HAP accountability principles. Output data were collected and shared more systematically, and in a more timely way.

In 2008, the Save the Children Alliance established a joint member policy in its *Rules and Principles for Alliance Emergency Response* (Save the Children, 2009) to evaluate emergency operations systematically within 6 months of a response, facilitate a lessons-learned exercise of emergency operations within 9 months of a response, and complete a program evaluation in line with ALNAP standards (similar to the Save the Children 2007 evaluation of the Batagram Earthquake response) for all large-scale emergencies. In 2009, Save the Children finalized a set of evaluation standards for all relief and development programs, focused on relevance, timeliness, and communications to understand performance, ensure accountability, and make quality improvements. Finally, the agency's operational standards for its international programs now include the monitoring and evaluation of emergency responses.

Although significant progress has been made, challenges remain, including the need to increase staff understanding of and adherence to emergency evaluation standards and guidelines and ensure adequate resource allocation.

Challenges in Evaluating Responses

Compliance With Sector Standards and Guidelines. The humanitarian sector has faced increasing pressure to respond to larger, more frequent, and complex emergencies, and to rationalize the numerous standards meant to guide their work. Many international organizations did not fully understand the ALNAP, HAP, and Sphere guidelines even years after they were created. Nor were many domestic organizations around the world aware of international developments. Although many organizations committed to and internalized international standards, they were uncertain of the system and resource implications of meeting and monitoring compliance with them.

The ECB project was initiated through discussions among seven NGOs in an interagency working group to help address some of these challenges. The *Common Humanitarian Accountability Framework for IWG Agencies* (Bhattacharjee, 2007) was drafted to bring various sector standards and guidelines together to help translate them into practice. This work informed Save the Children's 2007 evaluation of its Batagram Earthquake response in 2005, the first evaluation the agency commissioned focused on compliance with sector standards (see Kirby, 2007). The evaluation found that although Save the Children's assessments lacked consistency with Sphere standards, program implementation met Red Cross and Red Crescent Code of Conduct and Sphere standards. This evaluation set an agency precedent for assessing compliance with sector standards and the roles that planning and preparedness play in an emergency response.

Following the 2008 hurricanes in Haiti, Save the Children staff reviewed compliance with standards and found inconsistent knowledge of Sphere standards and varying degrees of compliance. For example, provisions procured for distribution met Sphere standards, but the ratio of latrines to children in all Save the Children child-friendly spaces did not.

Save the Children's recently drafted accountability framework incorporates the various sector standards to guide agency initiatives, and will be used to "ensure staff are aware of technical standards and guidelines and have a plan to reach them as applicable." In addition, the emergency response management sector in the United States is developing domestic guidelines and standards, distinct from international standards. Save the Children's experience in adhering to Sphere standards internationally is helping inform this work. Still, challenges remain to guarantee standards are applied appropriately and staff are adequately and continually trained.

Participation of Local Affected Populations in Assessment, Design, Monitoring, and Evaluation. Evaluations of Save the Children's earlier responses (e.g., Iraq, Darfur) do not explicitly highlight the participation of locally affected populations in assessments or evaluation. The 2005 Hurricane Katrina response informally involved members from affected communities in the design, implementation, and evaluation of the disaster response. That same year, the Batagram Earthquake response included children in the implementation of child-friendly spaces and in some cases program design. That evaluation also included beneficiary perspectives through interviews with men, women, and children affected by the response. Evaluation findings highlighted the need to incorporate beneficiaries more consistently, particularly women, in program needs assessments and implementation to ensure the relevance and appropriateness of relief and recovery actions.

In recent years, Save the Children's international experience in this area has varied:

- Following the tsunami (2004), Save the Children established a mechanism whereby beneficiaries could ask questions, register complaints, or provide feedback on relief efforts. As one staff member noted, "We found that the process of investigation actually improved our relationship with the community (members)—it was a chance to demonstrate the respect we had for them."
- Cyclone Sidr in Bangladesh (2007) highlighted the positive effects and importance of community engagement, in which the SC-sponsored, community-led disaster risk-reduction activities prior to the cyclone may have helped save thousands of lives.
- In Myanmar following Cyclone Nargis (2008), Save the Children established mechanisms including information centers at every distribution point, and systems to gather feedback from children, across all programs. Many of these practices have continued throughout recovery programming.
- The review following the 2008 hurricanes in Haiti found that Save the Children staff consultation with residents in assessment, design, and implementation was stronger in some communities than others.
- Save the Children's 2009 responses in the West Bank and Gaza and Pakistan have established feedback loops and complaint mechanisms in the communities where the agency worked.

Globally, through simulations and risk-reduction planning with Save the Children, community members—both children and adults—are leading efforts to reduce their vulnerabilities to natural and man-made disasters. These approaches increase community ownership and the likelihood of a more transparent and relevant response, and in turn greater accountability to beneficiaries. Additionally, monitoring and evaluation done as part of preparedness and risk-reduction efforts provide reference points for measuring improvements in these areas over time and/or in comparison to other geographic locations with similar contexts.

Remaining challenges include: ensuring beneficiaries participate in emergency response and evaluation in ways that do not reinforce harmful power structures or expose them to even greater risk, and ensuring evaluations consider the ability of affected populations to return to "normal" or

NEW DIRECTIONS FOR EVALUATION • DOI: 10.1002/ev

even "better than normal." Continued rollout of the ECB-developed "Good Enough" approach will be key to ensure that, even in challenging contexts, staff take initial, practical steps toward ensuring accountability to disaster-affected people. In *The Good Enough Guide* (2007), being good enough is defined as "choosing the simple solution rather than the elaborate one. Good enough does not mean second best: it means acknowledging that in an emergency response, adopting a quick and simple approach to impact measurement and accountability may be the only practical possibility. When the situation changes you should aim to review your chosen solution and amend your approach accordingly." However, *The Good Enough Guide* does not contain comprehensive evaluation standards; it assumes that once the situation has stabilized, sector evaluation standards and norms apply.

Ensuring Appropriate Rigor in Method and Level of Measurement. A common perception of emergency evaluation across the sector is that expense and time requirements are barriers to evaluating impact. It would follow that evaluations of larger responses, particularly in terms of dollars raised, would focus on impact, beyond outputs or outcomes. Yet organizations have done relatively little evaluation of the broader social, economic, political, environmental, legal, or technological impact of major disaster responses. Additionally, more consistent and appropriate evaluations of medium- and small-scale responses are needed, but limited agency resources and capacities make this difficult. Priority is still given to large-scale emergencies, as smaller responses often translate into smaller budgets that do not always include evaluation.

Despite improvement efforts within the sector, including those of the UN and Red Cross, many still feel today that measuring outputs, delivered with beneficiary involvement and good coordination across the sector, would be a considerable accomplishment. Why? Measuring more than outputs and outcomes is difficult; it takes more time to realize impact than a typical "emergency response phase" allows; measuring changes in populations and society beyond those directly reached requires a different approach from that which is typically applied in an emergency response evaluation.

The tsunami (2004) marked the largest response in Save the Children's history in terms of dollars programmed. Although Save the Children has conducted various evaluations throughout the tsunami response and recovery phases, measuring the real impact of the response proves challenging. Results achievement does not always correlate with affected populations' satisfaction. Perceptions about program relevance, delivery, and results may vary dramatically, depending on who is asked. Still, the agency recognizes the opportunity that on-the-ground presence prior to, during, and following an emergency presents. Save the Children's scoping of an impact evaluation of the tsunami response in 2009 surfaced critical questions including: "What is meant by impact?" "Who defines it?" "What are the related implications?"

NEW DIRECTIONS FOR EVALUATION • DOI: 10.1002/ev

The second phase of the ECB project commenced in 2008 and holds promise in working to increase international response capacity not only at field level, but at agency and sector levels as well. One goal of ECB 2 is to strengthen sectorwide coordination with tools and training to implement sector standards and guidelines, and match academic research agendas with implementing agency evaluation agendas (CARE, on behalf of the Interagency Working Group, 2008).

Utilization of Evaluation and Learning

Learning Systems. The scale and complexity of Save the Children's responses to the emergencies in Iraq and Darfur in 2003 and 2004 required leveraging systems and staff from across the organization. In light of this, Save the Children conducted its first postresponse learning exercises involving staff beyond the "emergency responders" in the agency's humanitarian response department. However, it was not until the tsunami and Hurricane Katrina that a more widely owned commitment to effective emergency response and learning emerged across the agency. Staff mobilized from across the agency to support the largest response in agency history (tsunami) and the first response in the United States in more than 60 years (Katrina), giving new meaning to the terms *surge capacity* and *cross-training*, and shifting organizational culture and systems.

Save the Children established agency emergency preparedness planning and evaluation protocols in response to learning from the tsunami and Katrina responses. Categories and topics covered in each learning exercise have become increasingly standardized, allowing assessment and comparisons of performance. The agency institutionalized learning through action plans detailing steps each department would take to improve and prepare for the next response, including clarifying and documenting roles and responsibilities in support of agency responses.

Use of Evaluation Findings to Improve Response Programs and Process. Save the Children's Disaster Risk Reduction work and response to Bangladesh's Cyclone Sidr (2007) demonstrate the value of evaluation and learning from past responses. For example, a key finding was the need for protocols to establish and coordinate relationships with local communities, governments, and other NGOs early on, and ideally prior to a response. The potential for preparedness planning to increase resilience and strengthen coping mechanisms, and in turn help to mitigate the impact of a disaster and save lives, was reinforced in evaluations of the responses to Hurricane Katrina and the Batagram Earthquake in 2005.

Since then, Save the Children has worked to prepare communities systematically in countries considered high risk for future natural disasters, including Indonesia, Sri Lanka, and other post-tsunami-affected countries. For example, agency staff worked with coastal communities and local partner organizations in Bangladesh to prepare for storms and flooding, including prepositioning relief supplies and rescue equipment, training local disaster management committees, and conducting cyclone drills for over 10,000 residents in the cyclone-vulnerable areas. As a result, Save the Children helped evacuate communities in the days before Cyclone Sidr struck, and began distributing relief items and assessing the most immediate needs of children within 24 hours of landfall.

Save the Children Alliance Coordination. The Darfur evaluation highlighted the need for more regular field coordination and better definition of responsibilities across Alliance members during an emergency response, an issue that persisted through the tsunami. Although fundraising coordination was stronger in the tsunami response, operational roles and responsibilities were still blurred. The Batagram Earthquake response evaluation found that Alliance members on the ground coordinated implementation successfully, but better coordination in preparedness planning was needed. This evaluation also recommended that a single Alliance entity be established to support emergency responses, with one high-profile point of contact and representation on behalf of all Alliance members.

Efforts to clarify roles and improve coordination and planning resulted in the lead-member approach used in the responses to Cyclones Sidr and Nargis. One member agency was preidentified to lead the response on behalf of all members. Although evaluations found both responses more effective than individually led member responses, they highlighted a need for more consistent and objective decision making from one emergency response to the next. Additionally, the evaluations highlighted that the lead-member model was contingent on the strengths and limitations of the one lead member. Although the single point of contact was achieved with this model, the Alliance was not leveraging the collective strengths of all members to maximize emergency response efforts.

Since 2003, Save the Children has moved from implementing somewhat coordinated, yet independent responses (Darfur) with limited joint planning (tsunami, Batagram Earthquake) to a member-led model (Bangladesh and Myanmar). And as of 2009, the organization has shifted to a centralized model for Alliancewide preparedness, risk reduction, and emergency response designed to leverage all members' strengths. For example, staff serve in a liaison capacity, coordinating efforts on behalf of all Save the Children member organizations in-country with the various UN cluster systems and other multinational humanitarian assistance organizations around the world.

Interagency and Intra-Agency Coordination. The tsunami and Katrina responses reinforced for the humanitarian sector that not coordinating was not an option. The joint TEC of the tsunami response (2006) found little coordination on assessments, implementation, and evaluation across the more than 300 agencies responding, with each agency focused on its individual accountabilities. In the years following the tsunami response, the UN Inter-Agency Standing Committee has established global leads of clusters of

UN agencies and other responding organizations to address gaps and increase response quality collectively in nine areas: nutrition, health, water and sanitation, emergency shelter, camp coordination and management, protection, early recovery, logistics, and emergency telecommunications. In 2006, education was added to the UN cluster system, and in 2007 Save the Children was designated the colead for this cluster alongside UNICEF.

Since the tsunami, the relationships Save the Children staff formed through the ECB project, including joint evaluations of emergency responses in Niger and Guatemala, have enabled interagency collaboration with organizations beyond ECB activities. Save the Children has continued to participate in multiagency assessments, reviews, and planning to inform recovery efforts, including following the Batagram Earthquake (2005) and Cyclone Nargis (2008). Save the Children has also joined with leading relief agencies and media organizations to demand greater accountability and transparency to those affected by emergencies as part of the Inter-Agency Working Group on Communications with Disaster Affected Communities.

The Katrina response reinforced the importance of coordination across international and domestic contexts both within Save the Children and across the humanitarian sector. Hurricane Katrina challenged the U.S. government's capacity to implement an effective response, surprising many in the domestic and international emergency response worlds. When Save the Children saw the response lacked adequate focus on the needs of children, the agency quickly mobilized. Organization staff had been working on developing and refining child-friendly spaces and psychosocial programs in emergency responses internationally. Evaluations and learning from international experience informed Save the Children's Katrina response, but their use was limited given the very different setting. Perhaps more significant, Save the Children brought staff members who had supported the tsunami response into the Katrina response, enabling the transfer of knowledge and adaptation from the international to the domestic context. Katrina also formed a bridge on the sector level, as international organizations in the UN, Red Cross, and NGO community, including Save the Children, were invited to lend advice and expertise to the U.S. government in mobilizing and evaluating the response.

The Katrina response also highlighted the importance of coordination across key domestic actors in the U.S. Save the Children did not have programs in the affected areas prior to Hurricane Katrina, and this was its first major domestic response in over 60 years; as such, Save the Children lacked relationships with critical actors—local community organizations, municipal and state government offices, the Federal Emergency Management Administration (FEMA), and the American Red Cross.

Following the response, Save the Children developed a domestic emergency response program including a U.S.-focused rapid deployment response team; a core set of program interventions; policy analysis, advocacy, and internal communications protocols; and important domestic relationships with key local, state, and federal actors for future responses. For example, in response to Hurricane Ike (2008), Save the Children partnered with FEMA to ensure an appropriate focus on children in the design and implementation of joint assessments of shelters. This assessment is now standard practice in all emergency responses FEMA supports with shelter management or oversight.

The agency also developed a program guide to support successful replication of psychosocial programs and child-friendly spaces in various country contexts and settings. Additionally, in coordination with the International Institute of Child Rights Development, Save the Children developed design, monitoring, and evaluation tools for both international and U.S. programs, enabling comparative evaluation and learning across geographies in the future.

Still, coordination challenges across the sector persist: Ensuring agencies can deliver on accountabilities and maintain a comparative advantage while engaging fully in collaborative partnerships and ensuring the sector does not compromise response timeliness or quality at the expense of coordination. For example, program startup was delayed in working with UN clusters in at least two instances—Cyclone Sidr (2007) and the Georgia conflict and response (2008); organizations came together on their own to develop a coordinated approach, which was later integrated with UN efforts.

Improved Emergency Evaluation Approaches in the Future

Despite an increased focus on transparency, accountability, and learning, there are still few resources and incentives for measuring impact and coordinating across the sector. There are few consequences for poor-quality emergency responses that do not meet sector standards or appropriately involve affected populations in assessment, implementation, and evaluation. All who play a role in humanitarian response (government, NGOs, the UN, the Red Cross, and the private sector, both international and domestic) need to hold one another accountable for improving emergency evaluation approaches overall. This will require the following:

- *Leadership.* Without clear direction and value placed by leaders on delivering results in emergency responses, no amount of policy making or training will translate into improved practice.
- *Shift in mind-set.* Agencies need to view impact measurement as one of the best ways to be accountable to affected populations and all stakeholders.
- *Systemwide commitment.* All humanitarian actors need to increase and meet the demand for higher-quality evaluation. The promise and obligation from donors and aid agencies alike to use their resources to

strengthen evaluation approaches is essential. Otherwise, wisdom remains the same—you get what you pay for.

- *Community and staff preparedness.* Working with communities on disaster risk reduction and preparedness efforts prior to and following a response can mitigate the impact of disasters and strengthen recovery efforts. In monitoring and evaluation, preparedness data should be used as a reference for gauging response and recovery efficiency, effectiveness, and sustainability.
- *Joint planning and implementation.* Interagency and systemwide evaluations are stronger and more likely to be used if agencies share ownership over the findings and follow-up actions. One way to build that ownership is to coordinate throughout, and even prior to, a response. Similarly, there is much to be gained from continued sharing across international and domestic lines, in preparedness, response, and recovery, including the need for better measurement and evaluation.
- *Behavior change.* Changing performance management behaviors takes time within one organization, let alone an entire sector. Examples and models from early adopters can go a long way in shifting awareness and attitudes, and better mobilizing the sector.
- *Agility.* Coordination can be process, resource, and time intensive. The sector needs strategies that can facilitate coordination and still ensure relevant and timely responses that incorporate good monitoring and credible evaluation.
- *Learning approaches.* Shared learning approaches can create an environment where evaluation is seen as a tool for learning and improvement from one response to the next.
- *Like minds.* Donors and partners who believe in coordination and strong evaluation and learning need to find one another and together can develop creative ways to support it.

These are the key lessons and drivers of improvements that Save the Children's experience highlights. They are no doubt general to all disaster response organizations working in the international and domestic fields. Save the Children is committed to continuing the cycle of emergency evaluation and learning to ensure improvements in practice, and to working with actors across the sector to strengthen coordination and evaluation. In turn, the quality of responses will improve writ large, thereby improving the lives of more children and families in the face of disaster around the world.

References

Bhattacharjee, A. (2007). *Common humanitarian accountability framework for IWG agencies.* Unpublished document commissioned by the Inter-Agency Working Group on Emergencies.

Braun, S. (2004). *Report on emergency capacity—Analysis for the Interagency Working Group on emergency capacity.* Unpublished document commissioned by the Interagency Working Group on Emergencies.

CARE, on behalf of the Interagency Working Group. (2008). *Emergency Capacity Building Project Phase II—A proposal to the Bill and Melinda Gates Foundation.* Unpublished document.

Code of Conduct for The International Red Cross and Red Crescent Movement and NGOs in Disaster Relief. (2004). Retrieved June 23, 2009, from http://www.ifrc.org

Feinstein International Famine Center. (2004). *Ambiguity and change: Humanitarian NGOs prepare for the future.* Medford, MA: Author.

The good enough guide. (2007). London: Oxfam GB Publications. Retrieved August 25, 2009, from http://ecbproject.org/

Kirby, S. J. (2007). *Emergency response to earthquake, Batagram District, Pakistan.* Retrieved August 25, 2009, from http://www.alnap.org/resources/erd.aspx/

Save the Children. (2009). *Rules and principles for Save the Children emergency response.*

Steering Committee of the Joint Evaluation of Emergency Assistance to Rwanda. (1996). *The International Response to Conflict and Genocide: Lessons from the Rwanda Experience.* Retrieved June 23, 2009, from http://www.reliefweb.int

Tsunami Evaluation Coalition. (2006). *Joint evaluation of the International response to the Indian Ocean Tsunami: Synthesis report.* Retrieved June 24, 2009, from http://www.tsunamievaluation.org

MEGAN STEINKE-CHASE is director of Organizational Planning and Change Management with Save the Children.

DANIELLE TRANZILLO is director of Contributions in Kind with Save the Children.

NEW DIRECTIONS FOR EVALUATION • DOI: 10.1002/ev

Zantal-Wiener, K., & Horwood, T. J. (2010). Logic modeling as a tool to prepare to evaluate disaster and emergency preparedness, response, and recovery in schools. In L. A. Ritchie & W. MacDonald (Eds.), *Enhancing disaster and emergency preparedness, response, and recovery through evaluation. New Directions for Evaluation, 126,* 51–64.

5

Logic Modeling as a Tool to Prepare to Evaluate Disaster and Emergency Preparedness, Response, and Recovery in Schools

Kathy Zantal-Wiener, Thomas J. Horwood

Abstract

The authors propose a comprehensive evaluation framework to prepare for evaluating school emergency management programs. This framework involves a logic model that incorporates Government Performance and Results Act (GPRA) measures as a foundation for comprehensive evaluation that complements performance monitoring used by the U.S. Department of Education as part of its Readiness and Emergency Management for Schools (REMS) grant program. A sample logic model for school emergency management is provided that can be adapted and tailored for use in local evaluations by any school district or school. © Wiley Periodicals, Inc., and the American Evaluation Association.

The authors wish to thank Ed Clarke, Clarke Consulting, and Sara Strizzi, U.S. Department of Education, for their insightful comments. Portions of the chapter are based on work conducted by the authors under contract number GS23F8062H, funded by the Office of Safe and Drug-Free Schools at the U.S. Department of Education. However, the authors are responsible for the contents.

Natural disasters such as floods, earthquakes, fires, hurricanes, and tornados can strike a community with little or no warning. Hurricanes Katrina and Rita in 2005 emphasized the devastating impacts that disasters can have on schools and school communities. In addition, incidents such as school shootings have traumatized and disrupted communities, schools, families, and most especially, school-aged children. The tragic events of September 11, 2001, also made it clear that in addition to planning for traditional crises and emergencies, schools must now plan to respond to other catastrophic events on campus or in the community. Developing and evaluating school emergency management plans are key components of emergency readiness for America's school districts.

In 2008, there were 97,000 public schools and 35,000 nonpublic schools in the United States attended by 49.8 million students, served by 3.8 million teachers (Keigher, 2009). Each school has a commitment to ensure the safety and general welfare of those in the schools, and to provide appropriate policies, procedures, and strategies to maintain safe environments. Because of recent incidents involving natural hazards, shootings, and other emergencies or crises, schools are conducting a comprehensive review of policies, procedures, and systems related to safety and security, including emergency management. As with many critical issues being faced by school administrators, safety requires building support for the initiative and conducting a thorough and systematic process to produce a quality plan for managing emergencies.

This chapter proposes a framework that involves developing and using a logic model to plan and conduct an evaluation of comprehensive school emergency management programs in elementary and secondary schools. Early education facilities, such as day-care centers, and postsecondary institutions can also adopt the key messages for emergency planning.

Evaluating emergency and disaster management activities in nonschool settings provides substantial lessons learned. School emergency management is a new development, and so there is no comprehensive framework for evaluating school emergency management programs. There are many factors to consider when developing, implementing, and evaluating emergency management programs in a school setting, including: preparing for multiple hazards, developing comprehensive evaluation plans following the four phases of emergency management, and collaborating with other school divisions and community agencies.

The federal context for school emergency management is delineated by the Readiness and Emergency Management for Schools (REMS) Grant Initiative under the No Child Left Behind Act of 2001. Through the Act, the U.S. Department of Education's Office of Safe and Drug-Free Schools (OSDFS) has taken the lead in school emergency management programs. Because this grant program is subject to the data collection and reporting requirements of the Government Performance and Results Act of 1993

NEW DIRECTIONS FOR EVALUATION • DOI: 10.1002/ev

(GPRA, 1993), OSDFS has also established GPRA measures and provided guidance to REMS grantees on performance measurement.

There is a clear distinction between performance monitoring and program evaluation. However, when contemplating the development of a comprehensive evaluation framework for school emergency management programs, the GPRA performance measures provide a logical starting point for articulating the desired outcomes of a comprehensive school emergency management program.

Context of School Districts and Schools

Schools are dynamic environments with unique characteristics. Students and staff constantly move from one part of the school to another when changing classes, going to lunch, or going outside for recess, physical education, or dismissal. Parents, volunteers, and vendors also visit schools throughout the day. Some schools may have more than one building on a campus. Many students arrive at school via public transportation, school buses, and private cars; they also walk or ride their bicycles. Most often, entrance to each school building is limited to one door. Schools serve students, staff, and visitors from varied backgrounds, including those with disabilities and those who are English language learners. During an emergency, schools and their partners need to be prepared to respond to the unique needs of these students, staff, and visitors.

Because schools are located in various parts of a community or geographic area, logistical considerations come into play. For example, law enforcement and other first responders may take longer to reach a school in a rural area than in an urban or suburban area where services are more quickly accessed. Schools increasingly serve multiple purposes for the community and provide diverse services. Throughout the day, an elementary school may also house a day-care center, adult education classes, or medical and mental health clinics. In secondary schools, the athletic and arts-related events attract area residents, and these events often involve travel to other communities. Frequently, the community uses school facilities, such as stadiums, gyms, and auditoriums, after school hours for various activities. During local emergencies, resource-rich school facilities often serve as shelters for displaced residents or as staging areas for distributing relief supplies and providing services. Each of these contextual factors contributes to the need for a standard set of procedures and policies to manage multiple types of emergencies or crises in any given school, at any given time, and on any given day.

Preparing for Multiple Hazards. Emergency management plans for schools are often developed and adopted at the district level. The complexity and frequency of different types of emergencies or crises may vary by school within one district. Thus, district and school emergency management plans should:

- Be created and strengthened based on the unique characteristics (risks, vulnerabilities, and resources) of the district and its schools.
- Be developed, practiced, and enhanced in collaboration with community partners, including first responders.
- Ensure the safety of the whole school community, including students, staff, and visitors with disabilities and those with special communication, medical, or physical needs.
- Reflect the principles of the National Incident Management System (NIMS) and the Incident Command System (ICS), a comprehensive approach to emergency planning and a framework for federal, state, local, and private agencies to manage incidents effectively and collaboratively with the use of a core set of concepts, principles, procedures, processes, terminology, and standards.
- Provide for all hazards, from low-base-rate/high-impact hazards (e.g., natural disasters) to high-base-rate/low-impact hazards (e.g., student injuries). Other hazards may include transportation (e.g., plane crashes); nonstructural (e.g., bookshelves, light fixtures); chemical (e.g., science laboratory chemicals); biological (e.g., infectious disease, contaminated food in the cafeteria); physical well-being (e.g., staff or student deaths); and student culture (e.g., bullying, violent crimes, intruders).

A Comprehensive Emergency Management Plan

A comprehensive emergency management plan must include policies and procedures that will address any type of emergency or crisis. Unlike some other federal or international agencies, the Department of Education (ED) outlines a framework for developing the emergency management plans within the context of the four phases, rather than three phases, of emergency management: Prevention-Mitigation, Preparedness, Response, and Recovery. Table 5.1 shows the goals and illustrative activities of each phase, which link or connect to the other phases. Together, all four phases form the foundation for a comprehensive emergency preparedness, response, and recovery, as well as continuity of the instructional environment.

Collaborations With Other School Divisions and Community Agencies. Depending on the scope and scale of an emergency, a single school district office or department may not effectively respond to an emergency or crisis on its own. Effective emergency management planning, performance monitoring, and evaluation require engaging in numerous collaborations. Thus, it is critical that a comprehensive emergency management plan and associated evaluation activities include key collaborators from divisions within the school district's intraorganizational structures, such as food services, public affairs, transportation, student services, and community liaisons. These divisions play an integral role in ensuring the safety and security of students and school staff before, during, and after an emergency. To maximize

NEW DIRECTIONS FOR EVALUATION • DOI: 10.1002/ev

Table 5.1. Four Phases of Emergency Management—Goals and Illustrative Activities

Phase and Goal	Illustrative Activities to Be Conducted
Prevention/mitigation: Address the safety and integrity of facilities, security, culture, and climate of schools to ensure a safe and healthy learning environment	Establish key community partnerships and assess identified safety and security needs and vulnerabilities. Establish communication procedures for staff, parents, students, and the media. Conduct a community and school assessment of potential hazards and vulnerabilities, as well as use existing data, such as crime reports for the school and community and an inventory of safety and security challenges. Assess current efforts being implemented by the school, such as substance-abuse prevention programs and safety procedures. Examine policies that are related, but not limited, to food preparation; building access; student accountability; and school and community assessments related to threats, physical infrastructure, culture, and climate considerations.
Preparedness: Facilitate a rapid, coordinated, and effective response in the event of an emergency	Identify needs and goals using the data collected in the prevention-mitigation phase. Establish emergency management policies, procedures, and plans for rapid response. Develop emergency management structure (incident command system). Develop and incorporate a universal design for students, faculty, and visitors with special needs to increase accessibility. Identify response roles and responsibilities, including lines of authority and emergency priorities. Coordinate communication among first responders, partners, and school officials. Conduct training for all partners, school staff, students, and parents. Conduct simulated emergency drills and exercises.
Response: Implement the emergency management plan	Activate the emergency management plan to include response action such as lockdown or evacuation. Deploy the resources of various partners. Activate communication plans. Work with community partners and first responders. Account for all students and staff. Make informed decisions. Accelerate the recovery phase.
Recovery: Restore a safe and healthy learning environment	Support physical recovery (e.g., school building facilities). Ensure that business operations continue (e.g., paychecks or vendor agreements). Facilitate academic recovery (e.g., continuity of the curriculum). Assist and sustain the psychological/emotional health of students and staff.

Source: Adapted from resources developed by authors with the U.S. Department of Education Office of Safe and Drug-Free Schools, including *Components of Comprehensive School and School District Emergency Management Plans,* Vol. 2, Issue 2 (2007). Washington, DC: U.S. Department of Education.

resources, it is essential that school districts collaborate with community agencies and partners, such as fire, police, and emergency medical personnel; emergency management and homeland security; public and mental health; local government (e.g., transportation systems); staff; community-based and national organizations (e.g., Red Cross); and, if available, active and nonactive military personnel.

The Government Performance and Results Act of 1993. GPRA is one vehicle that the Education Department uses to obtain performance measurement data on the funded REMS grants. It focuses on describing results to improve accountability for expenditures from public funds. GPRA descriptive information helps inform congressional decision making by using systematically collected information. Each federal agency must state the intended accomplishments, identify the resources required, and periodically report to Congress.

The REMS grant program is subject to the data collection and performance reporting requirements of GPRA, and consequently has its own GPRA measures. When developing and implementing a comprehensive evaluation framework for school emergency management programs, these performance measures may provide a logical starting point for articulating the desired outcomes of the program. Notably, however, they may not be sufficient to explain why the outcomes described have occurred—this is the task of evaluation.

GPRA measures for the REMS program have focused on the number of hazards addressed, whether school personnel and partners demonstrated improved knowledge about emergency procedures for schools, and pre-planning to improve and sustain emergency plans continuously once federal funding ceases. Sample measures include the percentage of REMS grant sites reporting that they have:

- Increased the number of hazards addressed by the improved school emergency management plan, as compared with the baseline plan.
- Improved response time and quality of response to practice drills and simulated crises.
- Improved knowledge of school and/or district emergency management policies and procedures by school staff with responsibility for emergency management functions.
- Planned for, and committed to, the sustainability and continuous improvement of the school emergency management plan by the district and community partners, beyond the period of federal financial assistance.
- Increased the average number of NIMS course completions by key personnel at the start of the grant compared to the average number of NIMS course completions by key personnel at the end of the grant.

Currently, only the last GPRA measure related to NIMS training is required for FY2010 grantees.

NEW DIRECTIONS FOR EVALUATION • DOI: 10.1002/ev

The Emerging Role of Evaluation in School Emergency Management Programs

Historically, evaluation of emergency management programs has not occurred at the school district or school levels. Rather, evaluations occurred at the community, state, regional, or federal levels, with little attention to the roles that schools play in emergency management. Since 9/11, school-based emergency management policies, procedures, and plans have emerged as a new field, as did the evaluation of all emergency and disaster responses and recovery efforts. The OSDFS within ED is taking leadership through its REMS grant program to identify promising practices of district and school emergency management plans through performance monitoring and program evaluation. REMS grantees must integrate evaluation activities into each grant to determine the extent to which objectives are met at the local level. In addition, OSDFS also encourages each REMS grantee to develop project-specific objectives and process and outcome measures based on data drawn from community safety and crime data, and school and community assessments. This process allows for feedback and continuous improvement, uncovers new information or consequences that were not anticipated, and involves multiple stakeholders in the process, which helps to create buy-in for emergency management planning (Argeris, Hill, Sinkgraven, & Strizzi, 2008).

Incorporating GPRA and Other Measures Into Evaluations of School Emergency Management Programs. More often than not, school emergency management evaluations are combined with collecting performance measurement data to report progress toward GPRA measures. Evaluators can incorporate the GPRA measures, including those currently used or used in the past, into comprehensive evaluations of school emergency management programs.

The primary challenge involved with assessing school emergency management plans using GPRA performance measures is that they do not explain local process, implementation, and impact outcomes that also can be measured throughout the various stages of design and implementation. GPRA measures are aggregated grantee site-level outcomes that allow ED to report consistent measures from one year to the next. Although GPRA measures are aggregated at the federal level, they are still good outcome measures that schools can use as part of their internal or external evaluation of emergency management planning at the local level.

All districts, regardless of whether or not they have received REMS grant funds, should develop their own objectives and measures to evaluate the efficacy of their emergency management efforts. Though not frequently used by ED staff and grantees, one way to organize this process is to develop and use a logic model to guide school emergency management program development, implementation, performance measurement, and evaluation.

School Emergency Management Logic Model. A logic model articulates the context, mission, activities, processes (inputs and outputs), and desired outcomes of a school emergency management initiative. Developing the logic model, in collaboration with the school district's divisions and community partners, is helpful because these stakeholders may have little or no understanding of school emergency management initiatives. Collaboratively, stakeholders can discuss the changes that will occur throughout the development, implementation, monitoring, evaluation, and sustainability of the emergency management plan. Thus, working with school divisions and community partners, the logic models serve as:

- A programmatic tool to identify the issues the emergency plan will address, the participants involved, the target audience, the context in which the plan will be implemented, and the strategies and policies that will be implemented to achieve specific outcomes.
- An evaluation tool (i.e., a resource for evaluators to design the evaluation and to frame evaluation questions and activities) that illustrates the relationships between a program's mission, activities, and outcomes, and the surrounding external factors.
- A continuous feedback mechanism that is useful throughout the development, implementation, and evaluation of the emergency management plan.

Figure 5.1 depicts a sample logic model that incorporates the GPRA measures for a school or school district to plan, implement, monitor, or evaluate emergency management procedures and processes outlined in the emergency management plan.

The logic model should be customized based on input from the school or district emergency management planning committee and its partners. This feedback is collected as part of the committee's broader, ongoing efforts to articulate a shared vision and establish priorities for the school emergency management initiative. The proposed logic model is based on work of other organizations in fields other than school emergency management (e.g., University of Wisconsin Extension Service, n.d.; W. K. Kellogg Foundation, 2004).

School leaders and evaluators responsible for designing, implementing, and evaluating the emergency management plan can conduct an orientation training about the various components of a logic model and its purposes, provide the sample logic model to the committee members and partners, and work with the group to apply logic model concepts to the initiative. The orientation should begin by relating the logic model to specific overall mission for a district- or school-based emergency management plan, as well as to outline a given situation and priorities.

The situation should explain the typical factors to be addressed by the school emergency management initiative. One of the major factors that the initiative addresses is the fact that geographic characteristics of the community may present challenges. For example, in rural districts, district facilities

Figure 5.1. Sample Logic Model for a School or School District's Emergency Management Program

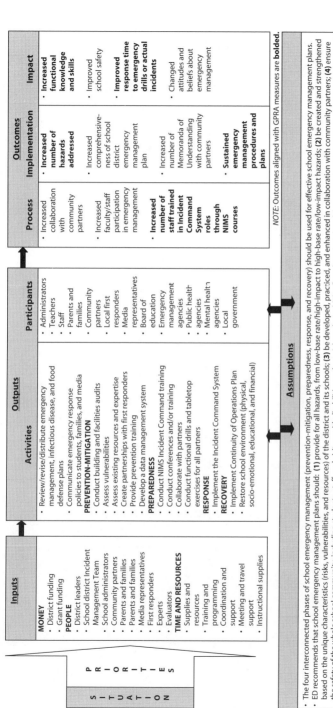

Source: Framework based on the work of the University of Wisconsin Extension Service (n.d).

and staff may be geographically dispersed, whereas in urban and suburban communities, traffic congestion may hinder the response time. Another major factor is that schools serve students, staff, and visitors from varied backgrounds, including those with disabilities and those who are English language learners. Other characteristics (e.g., location, size, extent of activities) of schools that should be considered as part of a given situation were previously discussed under the context of school districts.

When discussing the priorities, it is helpful to describe the main goals and objectives of the emergency management initiative. For example, a school district may have strong partnerships with local first-responder agencies, but may need to create opportunities for an individual school's personnel to develop partnerships with other community partners. Such an approach aims to prevent and mitigate all hazards, to use vulnerability assessments to create a tailored emergency management plan, and to have the systems in place to respond to a school-based incident.

Program inputs can be divided into money, people, and time—the resources that are invested in the emergency management initiative. Financial support comes primarily from the district or through grant funding. People include district leaders, the school and district Incident Management Team, school administrators, community partners, parents and families, media representatives, first responders, experts, and evaluators. The time and resources that people put into the program includes programming, coordination with each other, meetings and training, and instructional supplies.

Different logic models break down outputs in various ways. In this proposed model, program outputs are divided into activities and participation. Activities are the components that make up the school emergency management initiative; participation includes the district and community-partner staff members who engage in various components of the initiative.

Outcomes are the varying levels of benefits, effects, and consequences expected from the program inputs and outputs. Outcomes can be immediate, intermediate, or long term (impacts). For the school emergency management initiative, process outcomes may include increased collaboration with community and public safety partners, enhanced faculty and staff participation in emergency management activities, and increased number of staff trained in Incident Command System roles through NIMS courses. Implementation outcomes might reflect an increased number of hazards and vulnerabilities addressed, improved comprehensiveness of a school district's emergency management plan, increased number of Memoranda of Understanding with community partners, and sustained emergency management procedures and plans. Impact outcomes may include increased functional knowledge and skills, improved school safety, faster response time to emergency drills, and changed attitudes and beliefs about emergency management.

Various assumptions or beliefs about emergency management planning are often factors that are outside the control of the school (e.g., political decisions, funding resource levels, social changes). Collectively, these assumptions, as well as the people involved, the methodologies used during program implementation, and other external factors, influence the processes outlined in the logic model.

The School Emergency Management Evaluation Matrix. Once the stakeholders agree on the components and contents of the logic model, it may be helpful to develop a school emergency management evaluation matrix that summarizes the evaluation question, indicators, data collection activities, and personnel responsible for gathering the data. The evaluation matrix may also include a data analysis plan and time line to monitor the progress of the evaluation. Table 5.2 displays a sample school emergency management evaluation matrix.

Conclusion

The development, implementation, and evaluation of school emergency management programs are confounded by myriad complex organizational and environmental factors. The four phases of school emergency management—Prevention-Mitigation, Preparedness, Response, and Recovery—contain a discrete set of activities. The activities in each phase link and connect to the other phases. Together, all four phases provide the foundation for a comprehensive emergency preparedness, response, and recovery plan. This also sets the stage for continuity of the instructional environment.

The task of school emergency management is relatively new, and evaluators lack a comprehensive framework for evaluating school emergency management programs. Moreover, because methodologies to evaluate emergency management programs for schools continue to be developed, it is important to identify, address, and resolve the numerous challenges that surround evaluation of emergency management planning in this environment. The GPRA measures and indicators established for a federal program that supports emergency management plans in schools provide a basis for understanding the critical process and outcome measures schools and districts should consider when monitoring and reviewing their emergency management planning efforts. GPRA measures may assess, and often provide insights into, the school district's or school's political, economic, and physical contexts and processes that should be measured throughout the various stages of developing and implementing an emergency management plan. All of this feeds into systematic evaluation that attempts to explain performance outcomes.

A logic model that incorporates GPRA performance indicators can serve as a useful tool to articulate the process for, and components of, planning, implementing, monitoring, and evaluating district- or school-based emergency management efforts with community partners and first responders. Professionals in other school district divisions and the community partners may not be familiar with the process of logic modeling. Therefore, it is important to orient school officials and community partners about the

Table 5.2. School Emergency Management Evaluation Matrix

GPRA Measure or Evaluation Question	Sample Indicators	Data Collection Activities	Personnel
What percentage of REMS grant sites demonstrate that they have increased the number of hazards addressed by the improved school emergency management plan, as compared with the baseline plan?	Number of newly targeted hazards identified through the threat and environmental assessments Number of newly targeted hazards addressed once identified through the threat and environmental assessments Number of hazards included in the original school emergency management plan, compared with the target number of hazards discovered during the assessment and review of school and community data	Conduct a community and school assessment of potential hazards and vulnerabilities Review existing data, such as crime reports for the school and community Identify and inventory safety and security challenges for each school Assess current efforts being implemented by the school, such as substance abuse prevention programs and safety procedures Examine policies that are related, but not limited, to food preparation; building access; student accountability; and school and community assessments related to threats, physical infrastructure, culture, and climate considerations	Evaluator School district personnel Law enforcement Fire
What percentage of REMS grant sites demonstrate improved response time and quality of response to practice drills and simulated crises?	Extent to which there is increased collaboration with community partners A quantifiable decrease in the response time during a practice drill or simulated crisis that was staged at the beginning of the performance period and the end of the performance period	Number of new interagency agreements or Memoranda of Understanding (MOUs) in place Conduct tabletop exercises Conduct simulated emergency drills and exercises	Evaluator School district personnel Law enforcement Fire Emergency medical services

Evaluation question	Indicators	Data collection methods	Data sources
What percentage of REMS grant sites demonstrate improved knowledge of school and/or district emergency management policies and procedures by school staff with responsibility for emergency management functions?	The extent to which there is change in the knowledge of school staff, first responders, and other partners about emergency management protocols for schools concepts, policies, and procedures Changed attitudes and beliefs about emergency management	Administer pre- and post-knowledge tests Observe the extent to which staff and partners use skill during tabletop exercises Observe the extent to which staff and partners use skills and knowledge during simulated drills and exercises Training records	Evaluator School district personnel Law enforcement Fire Emergency medical services
What percentage of REMS grant sites have a plan for, and commitment to, the sustainability and continuous improvement of the school emergency management plan by the district and community partners, beyond the period of federal financial assistance?	Emergency management plan includes coordination with first responders and community partners Revised and enhanced comprehensive emergency management plan	Memoranda of Understanding Time lines Agendas for upcoming community partner meetings and drills, or school-board commitments to upcoming emergency management work or facilities upgrades that demonstrate plans to sustain and update the plan on an annual basis Existence of continuity-of-operations plan for business and academic recovery Plans for physical recovery of buildings Plans to assist and sustain the psychological/emotional health of students and staff	Evaluator School district personnel Law enforcement Fire Emergency medical services
What is the average number of National Incident Management System (NIMS) courses completed by key personnel at the start of the grant compared with the average number of NIMS course completions by key personnel at the end of the grant?	Number and types of courses taken Increase in number of staff trained in Incident Command System roles through NIMS courses	Documentation such as course certificates, sign-in sheets, or certification of attendance	Evaluator School district personnel

logic model and how to use it to develop, enhance, implement, monitor, and evaluate school emergency planning efforts associated with community emergency planning. To operationalize the logic model, an emergency management assessment matrix can be used to identify concrete planning and evaluation activities and time lines that all partners will share. Starting with an emergency-oriented logic model—and applying the lessons learned in this issue—should help facilitate the desired outcome of emergency readiness for a school district or school and support systematic evaluation of its potential and actual impact in the event of a disaster.

References

Argeris, E., Hill, T., Sinkgraven, M., & Strizzi, S. (2008). *Monitoring and evaluation: Site visits, reporting, and the Government Performance and Results Act.* Retrieved from http://rems.ed.gov/views/documents/Training_WADC08_PerformanceReporting GPRA.pdf

Government Performance and Results Act of 1993, Pub. L. No. 103–62, 107 Stat. 285.

Keigher, A. (2009). *Characteristics of public, private, and Bureau of Indian Education elementary and secondary schools in the United States: Results from the 2007–08 Schools and Staffing Survey* (NCES 2009–321). U.S. Department of Education, National Center for Education Statistics, Institute of Education Sciences.

University of Wisconsin Extension Service. (n.d.). *Enhancing program performance with logic models.* Madison: University of Wisconsin Extension Service. Retrieved from http://www.uwex.edu/ces/lmcourse

W. K. Kellogg Foundation. (2004). *Using logic models to look at evaluation: Logic model development guide.* Battle Creek, MI: Kellogg Foundation.

KATHY ZANTAL-WIENER *is a senior program associate at Synergy Enterprises, Inc., in Silver Spring, Maryland; she is the former director of the U.S. Department of Education's Emergency Response and Crisis Management Technical Assistance Center.*

THOMAS J. HORWOOD *is a manager at ICF International in Fairfax, Virginia; he is a former senior research associate and deputy director of the U.S. Department of Education's Emergency Response and Crisis Management Technical Assistance Center.*

NEW DIRECTIONS FOR EVALUATION • DOI: 10.1002/ev

Janis, A., Stiefel, K. M., & Carbullido, C. C. (2010). Evolution of a monitoring and evaluation system in disaster recovery: Learning from the Katrina Aid Today National Case
Management Consortium. In L. A. Ritchie & W. MacDonald (Eds.), *Enhancing disaster
and emergency preparedness, response, and recovery through evaluation. New Directions for
Evaluation, 126,* 65–77.

6

Evolution of a Monitoring and Evaluation System in Disaster Recovery: Learning From the Katrina Aid Today National Case Management Consortium

Amanda Janis, Kelly M. Stiefel, Celine C. Carbullido

Abstract

*Based on their personal experience and reflections, the authors describe and ana-
lyze the monitoring and evaluation system employed by Katrina Aid Today
(KAT), a program created by a consortium of partner agencies to provide disaster recovery case management services throughout the United States. In 2005,
Hurricane Katrina devastated communities along the U.S. Gulf Coast and displaced scores of people on a scale previously unknown in the United States. The
authors' reflections on the KAT model provide suggestions for future evaluations
of disaster case management. The need for flexibility in disaster recovery, monitoring and evaluation program design, critical aspects for implementing and
adapting an interagency monitoring and evaluation system, evolving interagency
data collection, developing outcome measures, and emphasizing program evaluation in disaster recovery are discussed.* © Wiley Periodicals, Inc., and the
American Evaluation Association.

Hurricane Katrina devastated the communities of the Gulf Coast in the United States on August 29, 2005, hitting the coastline states of Louisiana, Mississippi, and Alabama. The hurricane's destruction created a displacement of persons on a scale previously unknown in modern American history. Families were scattered throughout the country, resulting in a great need for long-term assistance and social support in order to achieve recovery.

In response to the large number and diversity of households affected by Hurricane Katrina, the United Methodist Committee on Relief (UMCOR), with funding from the Federal Emergency Management Agency (FEMA), created a unified consortium of agencies providing disaster recovery case management services. Between October 2005 and March 2008, Katrina Aid Today (KAT) operated as a coordinated social service network based on a model that emerged following 9/11. As such, KAT established its consortium as a multiorganization, multistate coordinated recovery intervention and provided case management services from December 2005 until March 2008.

KAT's programmatic design included a shared on-line database, standardized forms and reports, technical and programmatic support in addition to the case management services provided by agencies. The consortium structure was comprised of one administering agency, nine national partner agencies (managers), 134 subagency organizations, and 16 local partner organizations (field offices). KAT quickly scaled up in terms of operation and staff to roll out a standardized program design and implementation plan among the multiple organizations and states of operations.

One of the core components of KAT, as stated in the original proposal to FEMA, was a monitoring and evaluation (M&E) system that would be used to ensure that the goals and objectives of this interagency project were being met in a transparent manner. The disaster response strategy of UMCOR foresaw the importance of monitoring and measurement for describing the performance of UMCOR and the consortium through reporting to FEMA and the wider public. This transparency would presumably foster continued changes through the program design, best practices, and lessons learned in an accountable and responsible manner. The proposal also stated that a "key strategy (of the M&E design) would be to weave and infuse M&E activities into all levels and aspects of the projects administration and implementation." KAT's original design included monitoring and evaluation as a central aspect of its structure and implementation activities, operationalized by the program's results framework, which standardized services and promoted accountability among the consortium's nine national partners and 134 program agencies across the nation.

The purpose of this chapter is to share what we believe are the important lessons learned during 2 years of implementing an M&E system in a disaster recovery program. We highlight five key lessons learned:

1. The need for flexibility in program design
2. Implementing and adapting an interagency M&E system

New Directions for Evaluation • DOI: 10.1002/ev

3. Interagency data collection—how it evolved
4. Developing outcome measures
5. Emphasizing program evaluation in disaster recovery

Katrina Aid Today's monitoring and evaluation system demonstrated a capacity to develop an interagency system in real time as learning and evolution took place. This has implications for other monitoring and evaluation systems that operate in the disaster relief and recovery sector.

Flexibility in Program Design

As with other monitoring and evaluation (M&E) systems, a results framework guided the system in outlining program components through the identification of a program goal, inputs, outputs, and activities (see Figure 6.1). This results framework was developed by a consultant prior to the program's start and was accepted from the program's earliest days. The unprecedented scope and design of KAT meant there was a limited frame of reference for the program. Thus, program targets included in the results framework had to be based on calculated assumptions and expectations. The primary goal of the consortium was to provide disaster recovery case management services to 100,000 households to help overcome the multiple recovery barriers caused by Hurricane Katrina. Unable to predict the recovery from Katrina and without other comparable disasters, the results framework could not easily incorporate program outcomes.

In KAT's model, case management was broadly defined as a complex process involving a skilled helper working together with an individual or family to identify and overcome barriers to recovery. This broad definition was meant to ensure that clients receive the same service, regardless of location or situation. What this failed to allow for, however, were differences between individual clients' situations and needs. KAT did not incorporate a differentiation between degrees of case management services, meaning the stages of the case management process from outreach to eligibility screening to information and referral to fully engaged recovery planning. The program target was only designed to account for the case management process in its entirety, from outreach to recovery planning to case closure. By separating components or degrees of case management, there may have been opportunity to create a framework to account for the coordinated services provided by the case managers and case management programs along each client's path to recovery.

Since KAT was implemented under a proposal and contract with FEMA, the program design did not include a control group. That is, it was difficult to determine how families not receiving any services fared as compared to the clients of the KAT program. Yet, if the program had differentiated more among the stages of disaster recovery case management, control groups might have been identified within the program for evaluation purposes.

NEW DIRECTIONS FOR EVALUATION • DOI: 10.1002/ev

Figure 6.1. UMCOR-Katrina Aid Today Results Framework

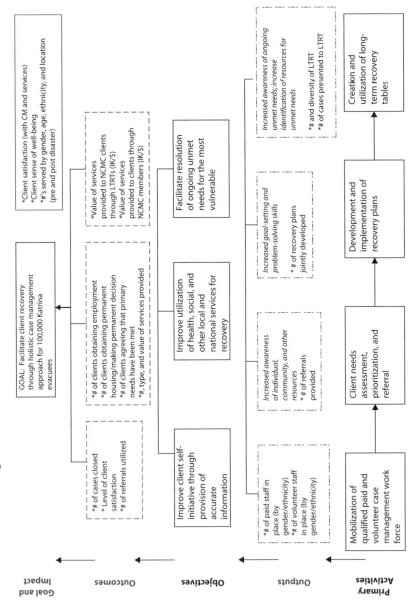

For example, it would have been possible to assess how families provided with information and referral (I&R) recovered in comparison with families assisted through recovery planning. In the future, efforts could be made in other recovery initiatives to help incorporate a full range of services under one coordinated program, such as the relief (e.g., debris removal, food delivery, initial assessment) to the recovery (e.g., home rebuilding, employment training, recovery planning). The outcomes or results of the program could then be tailored to the individual services that were provided, rather than to a single definition of service delivery.

In addition to the internal elements of a program, disaster recovery occurs in an environment with local and national influences. This impacts how, at what stage in the process, and where, recovery resources will unfold. These influences make the trajectory of disaster recovery unpredictable. Moreover, they present challenges in developing realistic and measurable programmatic benchmarks or evaluative indicators. For example, resources dedicated to Hurricane Katrina recovery, such as financial grants for repairs/rebuilds to damaged dwellings, were rolled out at a local level. They were implemented through the use of long-term recovery committees (LTRCs) rather than at a state or national level. This translated into inconsistent guidelines, forms, and available resources in different areas. Assisting the recovery of clients in such an unpredictable environment limits the use of measurable recovery benchmarks such as obtaining funds for the purpose of attaining recovery. Given these varying influences, the consortium was limited from using outcome measurements, as they were not yet established or standardized. This in turn limited evaluative efforts of KAT and similar programs.

Reflecting on KAT as a case example, future programs of similar effort and scope should operate from more informed service projections, as well as build into the evaluation design the elements that reflect the unpredictable nature of disaster recovery. One could anticipate that the implementation of a program will be prolonged, given the scale of the disaster and the scope of the program, and thus target outcomes should account for such.

Implementing and Adapting an Interagency M&E System

KAT's M&E system was designed by an external evaluation consultant and was implemented by the program's internal M&E team. The evaluation consultant anticipated core components, such as shared technology and reporting templates, but operational issues, such as the level of needed technical assistance by the consortium partners, were largely unforeseen. UMCOR had expected partners to have M&E capacity in-house. Instead, most of the KAT partners only allocated money for mid-term or final evaluations. As a result, the KAT M&E system was very hierarchical. National partners and local agencies were reliant upon the direction and design of the M&E system set forth by UMCOR for this specific project. The benefit of this structure was that all performance-monitoring information was shared with the field in a consistent manner; however, this implied that M&E functions were often layered upon other job functions and competed with staff persons' other responsibilities. Thus, the quality in M&E functions had to be emphasized continually in the form of technical assistance by KAT's M&E team.

Interagency Reporting. KAT's M&E system used quarterly reports to collect quantitative and qualitative data of current and planned activities, including any implementation challenges, and recommendations for improving the consortium from the partners' perspective. These quarterly reports were submitted by the agency to their national partner, who in turn consolidated the reports (ranging from 7 field offices to more than 20 field offices). One report was submitted to the M&E team at UMCOR from each national partner. The national partner reports were further consolidated and submitted to FEMA on a quarterly basis according to the donor reporting requirements. From start to finish, the quarterly reporting process took less than 30 days, as the reports worked their way from the agency to partner to UMCOR to FEMA. Without a standardized reporting process in place, this single report to FEMA would not only have been difficult to construct, but its content would have been inconsistent and unable to meet the donor or program management needs. A standardized report template would communicate expectations, enable uniform content, and fulfill responsibility to donors. Given the disaster field's dynamic environment and an agency focus on meeting clients' basic needs, a standardized reporting template may be the only way to ensure adequate reporting of the implemented work.

Shared Technology. One unique aspect of the KAT M&E system was the consortium's use of shared Web-based technology. The CAN database was developed by a consortium of agencies, led by the American Red Cross following 9/11, and communicates and documents services that are provided to disaster-impacted individuals in a coordinated and systematic way. CAN was used by KAT for service coordination, data collection, and program documentation. In order to ensure the database was consistent across the KAT consortium, KAT partners were contractually required to use CAN on a weekly basis for recording all client services.

The CAN database allowed for the sharing of information among KAT partners and between case managers in different states. This technology enabled case managers to record client information and case management indicators, ranging from basic demographics to the outcome of each client's case, electronically. Sharing a database has also proven its efficacy when dealing with the transient nature of the Katrina-impacted population, largely subjected to displacement, evacuations, and relocations. If a client moved to a different part of the country, any disaster recovery agency with access to CAN, whether part of KAT or not, could see what was provided to the client, whether the client's needs were met by the previous agency, or what unmet needs remained. For KAT, CAN mitigated the duplication of services and supported the continuity of relief support.

CAN served as the primary source of data to monitor, analyze, and evaluate the indicators set forth in the program's results framework at both the local agency individually and national level collectively. CAN allowed raw data to be exported uniformly to participating partners or agencies, based on criteria selected by the user. It also improved the accuracy and completeness of specific case management indicators that were critical to communicating the impact of KAT's programmatic work.

In addition to exporting data, CAN also provided the KAT leadership team with a range of reports that were available through a password-protected website that allowed up-to-the-minute status of the KAT caseload (i.e., percentage of open cases, services provided, etc). These reports provided the leadership team with accurate and accessible information and in turn permitted program results to be easily communicated to donor and other stakeholders.

In the early stages of program implementation and operation, the on-line database posed serious challenges for case manager users. KAT case managers were not only responsible for meeting with clients face to face, but ensuring that forms were completed and data entered from these forms into CAN—correctly, completely, and weekly. Included in KAT's implementation training was CAN training for all KAT case managers. To support these initial trainings, field visits were made by the KAT M&E team to review individualized caseload reports in order to identify where improvement in the data process could be made. Eventually, a few agencies hired data-entry support staff in meeting the data responsibilities, which proved effective for program evaluation purposes.

Shared technology has emerged as a permanent fixture in the disaster field's relief and recovery efforts given the need for up-to-date communication and coordination among multiple service providers. The CAN reporting technology used by KAT's M&E system stands as a solid example of how a shared on-line database can enable interagency programs to provide services in a more coordinated way.

Technical Assistance. Ongoing technical assistance provided by the KAT M&E team proved essential in establishing the program's standardized case management process and M&E system. This was critical given the compressed time line of the disaster recovery program. The first activity of the M&E team was to host a kick-off workshop to educate the national partners on the basics of monitoring and evaluation and introduce the M&E tools specific to the KAT program. Providing technical assistance continued throughout the project as both M&E functions and tools evolved.

The technical assistance provided included hands-on training such as field visits, informal one-on-one database training sessions, topical conference calls, and webinars. This mix of in-person and technology-driven assistance was necessary since the consortium operated throughout 34 states. Recognizing a need to regularly update and review CAN-specific issues, KAT instituted a conference call with agency-designated CAN points of contact. The purpose of the calls was to instruct agency-designated personnel on relevant CAN updates and discussions of the technological components of KAT's work.

Recognizing the opportunity to engage agencies in person, M&E site visits were made throughout the program. The report following each visit provided feedback on areas of strength and areas of needed improvement. The reports also gave a mechanism to remind the agency to follow up on the recommendations made during the site visit.

In addition to hands-on activities, technical assistance was also offered through a variety of written communications to establish uniform processes for case management and M&E functions. This included the development of a series of program guidance documents listing updated program policies and recommendations. These documents were developed as issues emerged that required a uniform response throughout the consortium. By the end of the program, KAT had developed 22 documents showing the program's shift through various implementation stages, from initial operations to closure. For example, an early topic for guidance was case-file organization, and later guidance documents addressed transferring cases and case closure. These guidance documents were an informal policy manual, which helped ensure that services were provided uniformly to clients no matter where the KAT client sought assistance. In a disaster recovery program of any scope and scale, technical assistance will be a cornerstone of a sound M&E system, as its components need to be constantly reinforced to program personnel that are appropriately focused on serving a population in critical need.

The Evolution of Interagency Data Collection

Although case managers learned how to use the program's on-line database during the first year of implementation, KAT primarily focused reporting on the progress of indicators listed in the results framework. These included the number of clients being served, the number of clients with developed recovery plans, the number of closed cases, the number of cases being managed by a volunteer, and the number of cases presented to the LTRCs to access resources for the client's recovery. Real-time information about program services allowed these indicators to be closely monitored, which was critical in improving the quality of data as well as case management services. For example, agencies reporting a low number of cases being closed were encouraged to review caseloads to determine if cases were being held open longer than necessary (an indicator of meeting social service needs rather than disaster-related need), or simply an opportunity to show agencies their data did not correspond to their actual caseload status.

Over the course of the program, case managers became more comfortable with the on-line database. With help from various data cleanup strategies implemented by KAT's M&E team, agencies began to view the database as a tool that could assist in their case management practices, which resulted in improved reporting. As a result, an evolution of data collection and reporting through CAN occurred. Data analysis began to ask questions such as: "For what reasons were cases closed?" or "Were closed cases successful in achieving their recovery plans?" or "Did clients feel their primary needs were being met?" By answering these questions, KAT was able to determine, quantitatively, if the program was assisting families in their recovery. To supplement this process, all closed cases, regardless of reason, were offered a voluntary and anonymous client satisfaction survey to complete. The survey consisted of open- and closed-ended questions addressing satisfaction with program elements, satisfaction with follow-up, staff knowledge and professionalism, and the level of recovery associated with receiving case management services. Survey results were aggregately compared with the data collected from the CAN database to gauge client satisfaction, case manager's assessment of the client's satisfaction, and the degree of client recovery following the case management process.

Once the quality and accuracy of data improved, the KAT M&E team started to analyze the relationship in real time between various Katrina impacts (e.g., whether a house was damaged, client had to relocate, client lost a loved one, etc.), household demographics (e.g., single female-headed households or residents of subsidized households), and the length of time a case was open or the reason a case was closed. These comparisons made it possible to determine the average length of time a case would need case management services to achieve recovery. It also helped to create benchmarks for future disaster case management programs. It resulted in an increased understanding of the amount of funding an agency would need to meet the case management needs of a household affected by a disaster. Whether special needs, household circumstances, or other recovery barriers existed for a family, these impacted the length of time for case management services and the amount of funding needed to provide these services. The evolution of data collection and analysis described above shifted the focus of KAT's M&E system from monitoring the program's reporting requirements to evaluating program management and design utility. This evolution also facilitated the consortium with a greater level of buy-in from the case managers and program managers. When partner and agency staff recognized the potential advocacy benefits of the data, the quality of data improved. Moreover, agencies invested themselves in the reporting of information for case management and M&E purposes.

Developing Outcome Measures

Because no other similar recovery efforts with published results prior to KAT existed, the consortium could not develop measurable outcomes or benchmarks based on prior research or experience. Although KAT's results framework set forth a number of indicators to track program activities, it could not be used as a tool to measure success on those indicators. For example, although the consortium was able to count the number of recovery plans that were developed, it had no point of comparison for what a reasonable expected number would be.

As with most disaster recovery programs, KAT was not specifically designed to be a pilot program with evaluation implications or responsibilities. KAT was not provided with data related to control groups for comparative purposes, but rather was funded by FEMA to implement a case management program. The KAT M&E team had an interest in researching recovery-related benchmarks and scanned sources for information related to benchmarking of Katrina recovery. Limited in nature, these sources singularly focused on recovery topics such as community rebuilding or post-traumatic stress disorders, which had limited relevance to the KAT model. Other sources, such as 9/11 or tsunami recovery, did not have a similar focus, and thus evaluative implications were difficult to establish. Future programs should be encouraged to look to subsequent programs for information that can serve as control groups to strengthen their evaluation process. With a lack of comparable data, however, the KAT M&E team recognized its potential to create outcome measures for future program designs. Although these data are only indicative of cases that were actively managed by the consortium, the experience of KAT may suggest the following baseline data from which future programs can assess program effectiveness and establish appropriate programming benchmarks:

- Eighty percent of KAT clients had a recovery plan developed.
- Seventy-eight percent of KAT clients closed for successful reasons.
- Eighty percent of KAT clients' cases were open for 100 days or less.
- The average number of days a KAT case was open was 213.
- Seventy-eight percent of closed KAT clients felt their primary needs were met.
- Caseload size was 41 cases per case manager per year.

Emphasis on Program Evaluation

To this point, the discussion of a standardized M&E system has primarily focused on monitoring. However, standardization also made KAT's evaluation activities possible. UMCOR, the administrating entity of KAT, included a formative midterm and summative final evaluation in the M&E system's design of the KAT proposal. Although the midterm evaluation focused on program management lessons learned to inform the second half of the program, the final summative evaluation attempted to document the consortium's impacts and model components with the expectation that they might have relevance for future disaster recovery programs. Both evaluations were designed to look at the consortium as a whole and the strengths of its structure under national partner agencies. In addition, several individual consortium partners implemented autonomous evaluations. This was to ensure that single-agency identities and results were not lost in the generalized, inter-agency lessons of the consortium.

During the implementation of the KAT program, FEMA was granted congressional authority to fund case management as part of future recovery services. This authority established KAT as a natural model for these future program designs. Understanding its relevance for future work, UMCOR sought to document its work in the final evaluation by addressing two research questions: "What were the impacts of the program?" and "What components of the KAT model should be used in future disaster recovery case management models?" These questions, in their simplest form, would help to identify best practices and lessons learned for future models. It was hoped that this would lead to defining the criteria for success, taking into account that each emergency has many unique elements that change from disaster to disaster.

Feedback from all layers of operation was sought during the evaluation. This included communications from the national and local managers, external stakeholders (LTRCs, FEMA, etc.), and clients. The consortium's standardized monitoring and reporting system made several sources of information available, including quarterly and client focus-group reports. The final evaluation also benefited from quantitative information from the CAN reporting system.

The KAT M&E system regarded direct feedback from the clients as one of the most informative methods of data collection. KAT sought client input in a variety of ways, including an optional client satisfaction survey given at the time of case closure, voluntary client focus groups conducted in 10 cities, and a survey sent to a sample of 5,500 client households. In seeking client input, KAT sought to learn if and how they had helped their clients and what more might have been done. Clients were overwhelmingly satisfied with the services they received from KAT. They described the KAT staff as professional and caring. They confirmed that the information they received was accurate. Overall, the message conveyed was the help received was the help needed.

As a federally funded program, KAT emphasized monitoring and reporting as an important means of transparency and accountability to the donor. The program also understood its unprecedented role and relevance to the field of disaster recovery. To this end, KAT undertook evaluation to demonstrate what worked well and what could be improved for future programs. The final evaluation implemented by UMCOR was a partnership between internal evaluators (M&E staff) and an external consultant group selected via an RFP process. The evaluation design was a composite, drawing from internal and external stakeholder input. The lessons learned from the evaluation can be used by other program organizations as they consider how their M&E design may include evaluation for both internal and general audience purposes.

NEW DIRECTIONS FOR EVALUATION • DOI: 10.1002/ev

Emerging from the KAT evaluative efforts was the consortium hope that additional research be conducted on the impact and delivery of case management services following Hurricane Katrina. Once the recovery efforts are complete, considerable information will be available for follow-on analysis of the costliest natural disaster in U.S. history. Such benchmarks will be useful in developing models and evaluative criteria for future disasters and case management programs.

Conclusion

The implementation of an interagency program, regardless of scope or size, must be flexible and adaptable. There is little doubt that interagency efforts afford advantages in disaster recovery over a singular agency approach. The expanded ability of multiple agencies working together to meet clients' diverse needs and share resources in partnership is not in question. So, too, M&E forms and reporting components should be standardized so that the information collected can be used for comparative purposes. However, the nonprofit or public agents implementing the program should still be able to express their cultural and/or programmatic uniqueness into the operational model. These programs should be encouraged to adapt the M&E system individually to their own needs and context, such as adding indicators or specific tools for tracking. Data must be in real time and supported by a variety of technical assistance sources to ensure that changes are communicated and replicated uniformly and consistently. Data specialists need to be hired to support this function, as monitoring data will be one of the strongest consortium instruments for communicating messages pertaining to unmet needs and resources requirements to congressional and legislative representatives with the power to implement change. The skill-set differentiation between case managers and data specialists is great enough to warrant separate staffing allocations for each.

Monitoring a disaster-recovery program such as KAT is rooted in comprehensive and quality data. Its availability has the potential to inform results-based performance management in real time. Additionally, its utility for implementing credible user-focused evaluation is clear. Monitoring data collected from an urgent disaster recovery program before, during, and after implementation is vital to determining progress and for evidence-based decision making. KAT disaster case management data offer a baseline for future comparisons. Further, future evaluations of disaster recovery programs may be able to draw upon KAT information in assessing future program operations. Developing more elaborate formative and summative evaluation approaches of emergency assistance programs such as KAT can better support understanding, capacity building, and emergency response programming practice.

The Katrina Aid Today program was the first federally funded disaster case management program. Although designed and implemented with few prior monitoring and evaluation references to draw upon associated with disasters of this scale, KAT was an opportunity to reflect on best practice and lessons learned. It was successful in designing and implementing a monitoring and evaluation system that may serve as a model for future emergency response efforts.

AMANDA JANIS is program director for the Disaster Case Management program of Catholic Charities USA; she served as the monitoring and evaluation manager for UMCOR-Katrina Aid Today.

KELLY M. STIEFEL is the monitoring and evaluation consultant for the State of Mississippi's Mississippi Case Management Consortium, the Disaster Case Management Pilot Program funded by FEMA; she was a senior monitoring and evaluation officer with UMCOR-Katrina Aid Today.

CELINE C. CARBULLIDO is a monitoring and evaluation consultant based in Washington, DC; she was a monitoring and evaluation officer with UMCOR-Katrina Aid Today.

Horan, J., Ritchie, L. A., Meinhold, S., Gill, D. A., Houghton, B. F., Gregg, C. E., et al. (2010). Evaluating disaster education: The National Oceanic and Atmospheric Administration's TsunamiReady™ community program and risk awareness education efforts in New Hanover County, North Carolina. In L. A. Ritchie & W. MacDonald (Eds.), *Enhancing disaster and emergency preparedness, response, and recovery through evaluation. New Directions for Evaluation, 126*, 79–93.

7

Evaluating Disaster Education: The National Oceanic and Atmospheric Administration's TsunamiReady™ Community Program and Risk Awareness Education Efforts in New Hanover County, North Carolina

Jennifer Horan, Liesel Ashley Ritchie, Stephen Meinhold, Duane A. Gill, Bruce F. Houghton, Chris E. Gregg, Tom Matheson, Douglas Paton, David Johnston

Abstract

This chapter describes the evaluation of the TsunamiReady™-based educational materials distributed in New Hanover County, North Carolina. The authors evaluate whether educational materials about tsunami risk increased the perception of hazard risk, information, knowledge, and preparedness behaviors. There are three main findings. First, local knowledge of regional hazards remains a strong predictor of changes in attitudes and behavior. Second, educational materials about unlikely hazards have only a moderate impact. Third, information seeking and preparedness behavior is a function of general psychological attributes such as personal risk calculations. The authors argue that a community's hazard experiences

and the frequency and severity of hazard events play an important role in recep-
tiveness to educational efforts as well as disaster preparedness. © Wiley Periodicals, Inc., and the American Evaluation Association.

This chapter examines community-level disaster and emergency preparedness. Specifically, we evaluate the effectiveness of a combination
of TsunamiReady™-based educational materials distributed in New
Hanover County, North Carolina, as part of a National Science Foundation
(NSF) grant assessing tsunami knowledge and preparedness in six U.S.
coastal communities. Using a quasiexperimental design, we evaluated
whether educational materials about tsunami risk increased the perception
of hazard risk, information, knowledge, and preparedness behaviors. This
approach is consistent with UNICEF efforts to evaluate the effectiveness of
public health interventions by examining changes in knowledge, attitudes,
and practices (e.g., see http://www.unicef.org/immunization/index_46109.
html).

Tsunami education efforts in the United States grew out of the National
Tsunami Hazard Mitigation Program (NTHMP), and until recently have
focused on the Pacific Coast (Bernard, 2005). The NTHMP made tsunami
risk education a national priority. A review of assessments in three states—
Oregon, Washington, and Northern California—found that awareness about
tsunamis had increased because of the program (Dengler, 2005). However,
that same review called for the "development and implementation of a uniform assessment tool to test the effectiveness of program education products and projects" (Dengler, 2005, p. 152)—a criticism that could be
directed at most disaster and hazard education programs.

Beginning in 2001, the National Oceanic and Atmospheric Administration (NOAA; http://www.tsunamiready.noaa.gov/) developed and implemented the TsunamiReady™ program, which runs parallel to the StormReady®
Community program. As of July 2009 there were 66 TsunamiReady™ sites in
the United States. The TsunamiReady™ program objectives are as follows:

- Create minimum standard community guidelines for adequate tsunami
  readiness.
- Increase public awareness and understanding of tsunami hazard.
- Improve community preplanning for tsunami disasters.
- Encourage consistency in educational materials and response.
- Recognize communities that have adopted TsunamiReady™ guidelines.

New Hanover County, North Carolina, is designated a TsunamiReady™
and StormReady® Community. Although the major hazards facing New
Hanover County are flash floods and hurricanes, the possibility of a tsunami
is real, even though there hasn't been one in recorded memory. People in
the county were not very worried about a tsunami affecting them prior to the
education campaign, but few of them knew what steps to take to protect

themselves if one should occur. We found that an education campaign can be effective in making people aware of tsunami risk, and of educating them in protecting themselves. The materials provided to them for tsunami education appeared to be effective, because most of the people who received them did not think it necessary to obtain further information on tsunami preparedness.

Evaluating Tsunami Education Efforts

Evidence from recent surveys in Oregon, Washington, and northern California finds an increase in tsunami awareness and hazard information among the general public in areas with an aggressive tsunami education effort (Dengler, 2005; Johnston et al., 2005; Karel, 1998). But there are two significant limitations to these previous studies. First, they focus on areas where there is a significant tsunami risk, meaning that in communities with very salient hazards there is likely to be greater knowledge of the hazard to begin with. This increased awareness makes these locations difficult places to study hazard education because of their hazard geography. That is, measuring a pre-education level of awareness, knowledge, attitudes, and behavior is extremely difficult because the hazard is part of local community culture. Second, the studies suffer from the common problem in social science research and evaluation of establishing causality. Most previous studies have not employed a longitudinal panel design, nor did they control the intervention content or exposure. Our chapter addresses both of these problems, community hazard culture and causality, by examining a tsunami education effort in a low-salience community (New Hanover County, North Carolina) and by using a panel study with control over the treatment content and delivery.

Study Location: New Hanover County, North Carolina. New Hanover County is located in southeastern North Carolina and is the smallest but most densely populated of the state's 100 counties. Its coastal location includes a number of eastward facing barrier-island communities, including the towns of Wrightsville Beach, Carolina Beach, and Kure Beach. According to the 2000 census, the county's population was slightly more than 160,000. In this geographically small community (approximately 200 square miles) this equates to a density of 800 people per square mile. Twenty-six percent of the county's households have children under age 18; 8% had residents over age 65; and 39% were nonfamily households. These demographics reveal a mixed population living in the county. Importantly for hazard planners, the county has grown by 15% between 2000 and 2008 (U.S. Census Bureau, 2010).

A rapidly growing and diverse coastal population presents a number of challenges to educating the public about hazards. First, the diversity of the population requires different education delivery mechanisms—younger demographics will rely on family caretakers and older demographics will rely more heavily on local government to receive information about imminent hazards. Second, population turnover in the area means that experience with the typical regional hazards is less developed. New residents can generally be expected to be less aware, less knowledgeable, and less prepared for typical regional hazards. Third, New Hanover County's coastal location draws a significant number of summer tourists. This seasonal population is important because of its size. During the summer tourism season local officials estimate that New Hanover County beaches have 100,000 daily visitors (Town of Kure Beach Hazard Plan, 2008, p. 2).

The most commonly occurring natural hazards in the region are flash flooding and hurricanes. Between 1996 and 1999, five hurricanes made landfall in New Hanover County. Since 1996, numerous other tropical storms either brushed the coastline or made landfall in the region. After a long period of drought, the spring of 2009 brought an increase in seasonal rains, leading to repeated episodes of flash flooding during the following summer. Less widely known, and certainly less salient to the public, is the area's tsunami risk stemming from the Puerto Rico Trench, Canary Islands, and continental shelf. In New Hanover County as a whole, 28% of the residents are relative newcomers, having located to the county in the past 7 years (the last time a significant hurricane affected the area was Hurricane Floyd in 1999). Meanwhile, 37% of residents have lived in the county for 10 years or less (the last time a hurricane hit the area directly was Hurricane Fran in 1997; these residents experienced Floyd). Among our sample, 60% of residents had lived "at the beach" for 10 years or less. Thus, 6 in 10 respondents had no direct experience with living at the beach when a Category 3 or greater storm makes landfall. As for tsunamis, there have been no events in living memory. The sample has a high socioeconomic status, with 64% of respondents having a bachelor's degree or postgraduate training, and 56% reporting household incomes of greater than $75,000.

Study Design. New Hanover County, North Carolina, was included as one of six locations in an NSF research project to develop a "tsunami preparedness model." The New Hanover County location focused on the barrier island beach communities of Wrightsville and Carolina Beach and included an educational treatment that occurred in between two mail surveys separated by 12 months (November 2006 and 2007). The educational treatment was deployed 6 months after the first survey (May–June 2007). During phase one, respondents from 448 households participated in the study for a 35% response rate. In phase two, 196 respondents (43% of phase one participants) completed the second survey. Most of the survey content was common across the six study sites, with additional modules specific to each study location. Ninety-nine percent of phase two respondents were the same respondent from phase one. After phase one, households were randomly divided into three groups: Group A received a tsunami brochure; Group B received a tsunami educational DVD; and Group C, the control group, received no additional materials.

Results. We were interested in evaluating the impacts of educational efforts on how respondents seek information about the hazard, what knowledge residents possessed or learned about evacuation routes and procedures, and finally, the level of hazard concern among respondents for tsunamis, coastal flooding, and hurricanes. Findings provide evidence that the educational materials had an impact on residents' attitudes about the level of risk they were facing. In the case of tsunamis, the impact has been to raise awareness for some, yet reduce it for others. Armed with knowledge about the relative risk of tsunami in this specific region, many respondents appear to believe that they are safe from an event. Others are concerned but not overly so.

Not Worried Before/Worried After. A key finding in previous studies is that hazard preparation is positively affected by personal concerns about the hazard (Green, Perry, & Lindell, 1981), willingness to prepare (Paton, Smith, & Johnston, 2005), and positive outcome expectancy (Paton et al., 2008). The premise is that individuals will be more likely to prepare if they are psychologically oriented toward taking precautions and if they can reasonably expect to prevent negative outcomes with their actions. But hazard preparation is also predicted by experience with hazard events (Gregg, Houghton, Johnston, Paton, & Swanson, 2004). These features of past research make our study location particularly interesting because there is no contemporary record of a tsunami event affecting the Carolinas (thus one might expect perceived risk to be low). Yet there is a small tsunami risk to the local area from activity in the Puerto Rico Trench, the Canary Islands/Cumbre Vieja Volcano, or a possible collapse of the continental shelf. Accordingly, it was not surprising when roughly one in four respondents in phase one believed that if there is a tsunami: (a) it will not be that bad (25%); (b) the location will be far away and have little impact on me (29%); and (c) the likelihood of a tsunami event has been exaggerated (17.3%).

Forty-one percent of residents believed that a tsunami was "likely" or "very likely" in the next 100 years. It is fair to say that the perception of the threat of tsunamis is relatively low. Although the frequency of hazard events alone does not predict positive behavior (cf. Paton et al., 2005; Paton, McClure, & Burgelt, 2006), it does have an influence. Moreover, our respondents have not experienced an event or a warning and are not overly concerned. Our interest is whether an educational campaign can be successful in this environment and whether concern about other local hazards can offset the lack of a tsunami in the community's collective memory. Although not the purpose of this article, we can compare these figures to the Pacific states, where respondents are more than twice as likely to be concerned. We would expect these individuals, for whom there is an important tsunami risk and therefore higher hazard awareness, to be most affected by the educational materials.

There are two important reasons to evaluate the effects of an educational campaign on residents where salience of the hazard is low. First, although

Table 7.1. Hurricane Hazard Concern

	% Worried
Category 4/5 hurricane will occur in 10 years	80%
Category 2/3 hurricane will occur in 10 years	96%
Category 1 hurricane will occur in 10 years	96%
Currently taking steps to prepare for next hurricane	74%

Table 7.2. Concern About Coastal Hazards

	% Worried
Tsunamis	51%
Hurricanes	97%
Coastal flooding	95%
Rip currents	99%

the perception of the threat of tsunamis is relatively low, New Hanover County residents understand risk and vulnerability related to coastal hazards, making them potentially susceptible to educational messages about tsunamis. New Hanover County beach communities are perceived by residents as a risky place to live. For example, data presented in Table 7.1 demonstrate high levels of concern about the likelihood of a serious hurricane affecting the area in the next decade. Almost all respondents indicated that a Category 1, 2, or 3 hurricane is likely in the area in the next 10 years, and nearly three-quarters are actively taking steps to prepare for the next hurricane. These responses are an unambiguous finding that residents understand the local risk of the region's primary natural hazard—hurricanes.

In an effort to understand better how risk across hazard types is perceived, we presented respondents in the phase two survey an opportunity to assess the relative risk to New Hanover County from four coastal hazards: hurricanes, coastal flooding, rip currents, and tsunamis. Information in Table 7.2 indicates that overall concern about tsunamis is less than half of what it is for hurricanes, coastal flooding, and rip currents. When asked to compare the relative risk, however, over one-half of the respondents said that they *agreed* or *strongly agreed* that "New Hanover County beaches are vulnerable to tsunamis."

Information collected in phase two of the panel design allowed us to observe the movement of individuals across categories of concern from one year to the next. Although question wording related to "worry about tsunamis" was not identical across the two surveys, there were comparable measures in both. In phase one, "tsunami worry" was measured by asking respondents to *disagree* or *strongly disagree* with the statement "The location of the tsunamis will be far away from here and have little impact on me." In phase two, respondents were asked to *agree* or *strongly agree* with the statement "New Hanover County beaches are vulnerable to tsunamis."

NEW DIRECTIONS FOR EVALUATION • DOI: 10.1002/ev

Table 7.3. Worried About Tsunamis

		Worried Before (2006)	
		No	Yes
Worried After (2007)	No	68 (65%)	25 (31%)
	Yes	37 (35%)	56 (69%)

Note: N = 186, contingency coefficient = 0.319, sig. 00.

Table 7.3 examines the relationship between "worried before" and "worried after" receiving educational materials. There was a significant positive relationship between being worried about the impact of a tsunami in both surveys. Sixty-seven percent of respondents were consistent in their opinion over time, but one-third (62/186) changed their view in phase two—with roughly equal numbers changing from *worried* to *less worried* and vice versa.

Fifty percent (68+25/186) of the residents were not worried about tsunamis or became less worried during the project. Previous studies suggest these individuals may be difficult to reach with educational materials. However, the remaining 50% either started out and remained worried or became worried during the project. Thus, although tsunamis are not automatically viewed as a high-risk hazard in this area, there is evidence that a sufficient number of residents are concerned to make a successful educational campaign possible. For the remaining residents, findings may suggest other approaches are needed beyond distribution of educational materials (e.g., town hall discussions, economic incentives, environmental regulations).

The second reason that we expect coastal New Hanover County residents to be affected by the education campaign is a combination of the Indian Ocean tsunami in 2004 and the mass media attention given to a possible collapse of Cumbre Vieja (a volcano in the Canary Islands) that *Popular Mechanics* in 2006 (Gorman, 2006) named as one of "5 Natural Disasters Headed for the United States." The article included the statement ". . .tens of millions of Americans from Key West, Florida, to South Lubec, Maine, have just 9 hours to escape with their lives."

Additional media reports focused on the possible catastrophe predicted from such a collapse, and it is possible that this raised awareness. New Hanover County had also begun taking the steps to improve its preparedness for a possible tsunami before the TsunamiReady™ community program was officially launched. Although public discussion was limited, it is possible that citizens had begun to hear about the tsunami hazard as they learned about other coastal events, such as hurricanes and flooding.

Relationship Between Worrying About Tsunamis and Educational Treatment. The unique nature of this project allows us to examine the relationship between worrying about tsunamis and the educational value of

Table 7.4. Educational Treatment Impact on Awareness

	Control	Brochure	DVD
Not worried	23	27	18
	28%	50%	35%
Became less worried	9	9	7
	11%	17%	14%
Worried	34	8	14
	42%	15%	27%
Became worried	15	10	12
	19%	19%	24%
Total	81	54	51

Note: Cells include only those respondents who answered to the tsunami worry item in both surveys and were part of the control or experimental groups.

receiving a tsunami brochure or DVD—a relatively simple evaluation of whether the program materials increased awareness of the hazard event.

Table 7.4 illustrates movement across categories of concern, as we saw in Table 7.3, but there are also differences across various categories of educational treatments (brochure or DVD). In each case the households that received the educational materials (brochure or DVD) were consistently different from the control group, exhibiting a small increase in the *became not worried* category because of the treatment, and a decrease in the *worried* category when compared with the control group. Of the households that received the brochure, 17% became less worried compared with the control group, where 11% became less worried. Among the households that received the DVD, 14% became less worried (compared with 11% of the control group), and 24% became more worried (compared with 19% of the control group). What is somewhat surprising is the erratic nature of the movement in the *not worried in 2006 or 2007* and *worried in 2006 and 2007* categories. For example, of the respondents who received the brochure 50% were *not worried* compared with 28% of the control group. We find clear evidence for increased awareness of tsunami hazards from one survey to the next, but untangling the effect of the exposure to the hazard by the instrument and the impact of the educational material is difficult. It is entirely possible, given the high socioeconomic status of the respondents, that once they received the first instrument they sought out information about tsunamis, which would have muted the impact of the interventions. However, the project did not allow for testing of such instrument effects. Next we turn our attention to whether the increase in concern, coupled with the educational materials, increased awareness and influenced behavior.

Seeking Tsunami Information. A key element of hazard preparedness, especially when there is little local experience and awareness is low, is the collection of hazard-relevant information. Research has shown that general information programs are ineffective (Duval & Mullis, 1999; Lindell &

Table 7.5. Information Seeking

2006	Respondents Who Plan to...	Control	Brochure	DVD	Became Worried	Became Less Worried
					2007	
9%	Improve knowledge of tsunamis	6%	9%	8%	24%	0%
12%	Increase ability to respond to tsunamis	8%	2%	6%	16%	0%
17%	Seek information on tsunami risks	10%	4%	4%	14%	0%
18%	Seek information on things to do to respond to tsunamis	12%	9%	2%	22%	0%

Note: The stem wording for both phases was: "In the next month or so, do you intend to do any of the following?" The cell percentages report the number of respondents who indicated their plans to seek information about tsunamis "definitely." The column and row percentages do not sum to 100% because there were other categories of possible responses. The "became worried" and "became less worried" categories are explained in Table 7.3.

Whitney, 2000; Paton, McClure, & Burgelt, 2006). However, the information campaign in the current project was targeted and specific. It was sent only to households that were in the high-risk zone (presumably receptive to the message) and was specific to the tsunami threat (the brochure and DVD video were compiled and, in the case of the DVD, narrated by an expert). Both surveys asked respondents about their intention to learn more about tsunamis. In the 2006 survey, fewer than one in five individuals reported plans to seek additional information. Interest in seeking additional information decreased in the 2007 survey and plummeted among households that received the educational materials. Fewer than 5% of the households that received a brochure or DVD reported in 2007 that they planned to seek additional information (compared with 1 in 10 in the control group). This is not an entirely unanticipated effect, as the primary goal of the educational materials was to increase knowledge about what to do in the event of a tsunami. The materials directed residents to prepare for a local evacuation away from the beachfront or to areas at least 15 feet above mean high tide.

For comparison, we examined the information-seeking plans of respondents who became more or less worried about tsunamis between phase one (2006) and phase two (2007). The final two columns in Table 7.5 show that in the 2007 survey nearly one-quarter of respondents who became worried planned to improve their knowledge of tsunamis and planned to seek information on things to do (slightly more than those who originally reported plans to do this in the 2006 survey). No respondent who became less worried about tsunamis had any plans to seek additional information. It is difficult to establish the exact causal mechanism that led to the drop in

Figure 7.1. Tsunami Hazard Signs

Tsunami Hazard Sign   Standard Tsunami Hazard Sign
New Hanover County, NC

information-seeking behavior among those who became less worried about tsunamis, but clearly the educational campaign had an effect.

Knowledge of Evacuation Zones and Plans. The greatest fear of emergency managers in New Hanover County is that a tsunami warning will occur during the summer, when local officials estimate the daily beach population to be approximately 100,000. Previous studies have documented the challenges of reaching tourists with hazard information (Drabek, 1996). Emergency managers are concerned that residents and tourists will try to evacuate the island, rather than only evacuate the ocean beachfront—which is recommended in most scenarios. The official evacuation zone for both beach communities in this geographical area is 300 feet inland and/or 15 feet vertically above the mean high tide. Thus, in the most likely warning scenario there is no need to evacuate the island. As depicted in Figure 7.1, when New Hanover County became a TsunamiReady™ Community it modified the standard TsunamiReady™ sign to direct people to "Evacuate the Beaches" in case of tsunami, rather than "Go to High Ground or Inland" in case of an earthquake.

Figure 7.1 illustrates a subtle but important difference. In developing the plans for how to communicate a tsunami warning in New Hanover County, considerable discussion was given to what language emergency management officials, town officials, lifeguards, and others should use. After considerable discussion, local officials agreed that "evacuate the beachfront" would be best. However, officials were concerned about individuals not understanding what the "beachfront" is, so the "evacuate the beaches" instruction became the default. This statement remains problematic because it is possible to confuse "evacuate the beaches" with "evacuate the island," but this will have to be resolved through the ongoing educational campaign.

Based on the survey findings from both phases, the distinction between beach evacuation and island evacuation is difficult to communicate to residents. In the first survey when respondents were asked whether they lived in a tsunami inundation zone, 90% said "yes" or "don't know." (See Table 7.6.) However, most do not actually live in an inundation zone. Respondents were also asked whether an evacuation zone exists; to this question only 12% said

NEW DIRECTIONS FOR EVALUATION • DOI: 10.1002/ev

Table 7.6. Knowledge of Evacuation Issues

	All/Pre	Control	Brochure	DVD
Tsunami evacuation zone exists	12%	18%	25%	25%
(yes/don't know)	53%	69%	66%	65%
Live in a tsunami inundation zone	42%			
(yes/don't know)	48%			
Evacuation requires:				
Leaving the island		61%	57%	58%
Leave only the beachfront along ocean/go up		18%	22%	12%
Don't know		21%	20%	30%

Note: The question about the tsunami evacuation zone in phase one is "Are there official tsunami evacuation routes for your community?" In phase two it is "Does a tsunami evacuation zone exist for New Hanover County beaches?"

"yes." In an effort to evaluate the impact of the educational materials sent between phase one and phase two of the study, the second survey included more specific questions about evacuation behavior. Both forms of educational materials stressed that evacuation from the island was most likely unnecessary. Knowledge that an evacuation zone exists was higher among both experimental groups but it is less clear how that translated into plans for action. Even after receiving the educational materials, more than 50% of respondents indicated they planned to "leave the island" if an evacuation order were called. This emphasizes the need to provide local context to an evacuation order; the nature of the tsunami risk in New Hanover County is different from the Pacific Northwest, California, Alaska, or Indonesia.

In each case the impact of the educational treatment was to increase the number of participants who responded "don't know." Substituting our measure of tsunami awareness for the experimental treatment does not change the results. Neither getting information about the tsunami hazard facing the area, nor being worried about it, appear to affect the likelihood of a planned evacuation of the island substantially. Although our survey primarily focused on residents it is reasonable to conclude that they are more knowledgeable about the hazard than visitors. Thus, there are considerable challenges that emergency managers face with respect to educating tourists.

Behavior Changes. The final section of this chapter examines a series of preparedness actions that were common across all six of the study locations in the United States. Although the behavior items do not require substantial actions or expense, it would be surprising if many New Hanover County residents took these actions given the relatively low awareness of tsunami hazards in the region. Recall, however, that nearly three-quarters of survey respondents reported taking action to prevent hurricane damage. Less than 10% ($n = 32$) of the 2006 respondents indicated that they were taking actions to become more tsunami ready. Table 7.7 presents the percent of respondents who

Table 7.7. Respondents Taking Action to Become Prepared

2006	Reported Taking Action:	Control	Brochure	DVD	Became Worried	Became Less Worried
				2007		
63%	Developed a family emergency plan	67%	63%	57%	71%	50%
77%	Have a 3-day supply of nonperishable food and water	75%	63%	71%	57%	100%
38%	Have a backpack filled with supplies that is ready to take with me	33%	38%	14%	29%	25%
71%	Have a NOAA weather radio and working batteries	83%	75%	43%	71%	50%
34%	Prepared to respond to tsunamis in more places than my home	27%	25%	29%	14%	75%
16%	Participated in a tsunami evacuation drill	27%	13%	0%	17%	25%

Note: Cell percentages report the number of respondents who indicated their plans to take action "definitely." Column and row percentages do not sum to 100% because there were other categories of possible responses. The "became worried" and "became less worried" categories are explained in Table 7.3.

engaged in various types of actions for 2006 along with comparisons for those who received the varying educational materials. The 2006 data reflect only those individuals who reported taking action to become more tsunami ready. In 2007, all respondents were asked if they had done any of the following in the previous year.

Overall, the level of preparedness among respondents reporting "taking some action" or "having taken some action" in the previous year is similar to data collected in Kodiak, Alaska (Paton et al., 2008; Ritchie & Gill, 2008), which is surprising given the difference in relative tsunami risk between the two communities. This finding is more likely a function of the fact that most of the preparedness items for tsunamis share the common purpose of preparing households for hurricanes. There appears to be a slight tendency for respondents who received the DVD to report lower levels of preparedness compared with the control group, but small cell sizes make it difficult to state any firm conclusions. The same conclusion generally holds for those respondents who changed their views during the project.

Conclusion

The most recent National Tsunami Research Plan calls for a strong emphasis on education (Bernard, Dengler, & Yim, 2007). Social science has been slow to evaluate the strategies adopted by hazard education programs within the United States. Research design issues and cost make such analyses difficult. The evaluation design presented in this chapter was created in collaboration with the local National Weather Service and emergency management officials in New Hanover County, North Carolina, to assess the effectiveness of materials developed to educate residents of beach communities about tsunami hazards.

This chapter makes three important contributions. First, we confirm that the salience or awareness of the hazard threat is an important predictor of changes in attitudes and behavior. Tsunamis are perceived as a low-risk/salient hazard event in New Hanover County, yet a significant number of people became concerned about a tsunami event during the course of the study—and exhibited a corresponding intention to acquire additional information about the hazard. We postulate that this is, at least in part, due to the overall high level of awareness of coastal hazard events (hurricanes, floods, rip currents) in the area and the impact of the tsunami hazard educational campaign. Previous research has focused on the idea that hazard events with low salience and infrequent occurrence are difficult to prepare for; our study suggests that a different kind of thinking might be in order. Overall, we found more respondents were concerned about the tsunami hazard than one would predict for an area that has never had one and has a low probability of serious damage from such an event.

Second, our evaluation of the effectiveness of tsunami information presented in a brochure and DVD format showed only a small effect on attitudes and behavior. Although these materials were targeted to beach residents and were specific to tsunami hazards, most changes in respondents' awareness and attitudes were limited. In one of the more striking findings, those who became less worried about tsunami events from 2006–2007 reported no interest in improving their knowledge about tsunamis or seeking additional information. It seems likely that respondents believed the materials provided were comprehensive and understandable.

Regarding the most pressing issues for emergency managers—warnings and evacuations—our study found that the vast majority of respondents continued to report, incorrectly, that if an evacuation order is called that they should leave the island rather than merely evacuate the beach or move to higher ground (or they reported not knowing what to do). Again, we believe that the local context to tsunami risk is lacking; thus, respondents may be reacting to knowledge about general tsunami preparedness and risk (e.g., the Indian Ocean tsunami), rather than considering the likely impact of a local tsunami event.

Third, this work confirms the general theoretical approach that views information seeking and preparedness behavior as a function of general psychological attributes such as personal risk calculations. Moreover, we argue that a community's hazard experiences—the collective memory—and the frequency and severity of hazard events play an important role in receptiveness to educational efforts as well as disaster preparedness.

The challenges facing disaster and hazard education programs are considerable. In particular, it is extremely difficult to compete for the public's attention, especially when the salience of the hazard is low and the occurrence infrequent. Despite this, emergency managers and hazard educators must be proactive in creating disaster-resilient communities and mitigating disaster consequences. Coupling these activities with sound evaluation efforts has potential to improve disaster and emergency preparedness, response, and recovery.

References

Bernard, E. (2005). The U.S. National Tsunami Hazard Mitigation Program: A successful state-federal partnership. *Natural Hazards, 35*(1), 5–24.

Bernard, E. N., Dengler, L. A., & Yim, S. C. (2007). *National Tsunami Research Plan: Report of a workshop sponsored by NSF/NOAA* (OAR PMEL-133). Seattle, WA: Pacific Marine Environmental Laboratory.

Dengler, L. (2005). The role of education in the National Tsunami Hazard Mitigation Program. *Natural Hazards, 35*(1), 141–153.

Drabek, T. E. (1996). *Disaster education behavior: Tourists and other transients*. Boulder, CO: Institute of Behavioral Science, Program on Environment and Behavior.

Duval, T. S., & Mullis, J. P. (1999). A person-relative-to-event (PrE) approach to negative threat appeals and earthquake preparedness: A field study. *Journal of Applied Social Psychology, 29*, 495–516.

Gorman, J. (2006). FUTURE shocks. *Popular Mechanics, 183*(10), 66–71.

Greene, M., Perry, R., & Lindell, M. (1981). The March 1980 eruptions of Mt. St. Helens: Citizens perceptions of volcano threat. *Disasters, 5*(1), 49–66.

Gregg, C. E., Houghton, B. F., Johnston, D. M., Paton, D., & Swanson, D. A. (2004). The perception of volcanic risk in Kona communities from Mauna Loa and Hualalai volcanoes, Hawaii. *Journal of Volcanology and Geothermal Research, 130*, 179–196.

Johnston, D., Paton, D., Crawford, G. L., Ronan, K., Houghton, B., & Burgelt, P. (2005). Measuring tsunami preparedness in coastal Washington, United States. *Natural Hazards, 35*(1), 173–184.

Karel, A. (1998). Oregonians need more information about tsunamis to save lives (results of a survey). *Oregon Geology, 60*(3), 56.

Lindell, M. K., & Whitney, D. J. (2000). Correlates of household seismic hazard adjustment adoption. *Risk Analysis, 20*, 13–25.

Paton, D., Houghton, B. F., Gregg, C. E., Gill, D. A., Ritchie, L. A., McIvor, D., et al. (2008). Managing tsunami risk in coastal communities: Identifying predictors of preparedness. *The Australian Journal of Emergency Management, 23*(1), 4–9.

Paton, D., McClure, J., & Burgelt, P. T. (2006). Natural hazard resilience: The role of individual and household preparedness. In D. Paton & D. Johnston (Eds.), *Disaster resilience: An integrated approach*. Springfield, IL: Charles C. Thomas.

Paton, D., Smith, L. M., & Johnston, D. (2005). When good intentions turn bad: Promoting natural hazard preparedness. *The Australian Journal of Emergency Management, 20*, 25–30.

Ritchie, L. A., & Gill, D. A. (2008). *U.S. tsunami survey: Kodiak, Alaska*. Collaborators Report.

U.S. Census Bureau: State and County QuickFacts. (2010). Data derived from Population Estimates, Census of Population and Housing, Small Area Income and Poverty

Estimates, State and County Housing Unit Estimates, County Business Patterns, Non-employer Statistics, Economic Census, Survey of Business Owners, Building Permits, Consolidated Federal Funds Report. Retrieved from http://quickfacts.census.gov/qfd/states/37/37129.html

JENNIFER HORAN is an assistant professor of political science at the University of North Carolina Wilmington.

LIESEL ASHLEY RITCHIE is assistant director for research at the University of Colorado's Natural Hazards Center.

STEPHEN MEINHOLD is associate dean of research and professor of political science at the University of North Carolina Wilmington.

DUANE A. GILL is professor and head of the department of sociology at Oklahoma State University.

BRUCE F. HOUGHTON is the Gordon MacDonald Professor in Volcanology at the University of Hawaii at Manoa and Hawaiian State Volcanologist and a Fellow of the Royal Society of New Zealand.

CHRIS E. GREGG is an assistant professor of geology at East Tennessee State University in Johnson City, Tennessee.

TOM MATHESON is retired from the National Weather Service (NWS), where he was most recently Warning Coordination Meteorologist, NWS, Wilmington, North Carolina.

DOUGLAS PATON is a professor in the School of Psychology, University of Tasmania, Australia.

DAVID JOHNSTON is the director of the Joint Centre for Disaster Research in the School of Psychology at Massey University, New Zealand.

Spence, P. R., & Lachlan, K. A. (2010). Disasters, crises, and unique populations: Suggestions for survey research. In L. A. Ritchie & W. MacDonald (Eds.), *Enhancing disaster and emergency preparedness, response, and recovery through evaluation. New Directions for Evaluation, 126,* 95–106.

8

Disasters, Crises, and Unique Populations: Suggestions for Survey Research

Patric R. Spence, Kenneth A. Lachlan

Abstract

Methodological and data-analysis challenges for evaluators working in disaster and crisis contexts are discussed. Crises are, by definition, unexpected, nonroutine occurrences that create conditions unfavorable to traditional methods of data collection. The inherently novel nature of disasters and large-scale crises, coupled with their unpredictability, often makes data collection difficult at best. Given the methodological limitations imposed by the conditions surrounding disasters, researchers and evaluators are often criticized for methodological decisions concerning data collection, randomization, and generalizability. This chapter addresses issues of data collection, randomization and data analysis in disaster research, outlining the difficulties of randomization, problems stemming from the absence of randomization, and potential solutions to these problems. © Wiley Periodicals, Inc., and the American Evaluation Association.

Evaluating disaster and crisis-related interventions poses significant obstacles to applied scholars. Those interested in examining the characteristics of disasters face a number of methodological and data analytic challenges. Crises are by definition unexpected, nonroutine events that often create conditions that are not favorable toward traditional methods of data collection. By their very nature disasters are crises of an exceptionally novel nature, and their unpredictability often makes data collection difficult.

Traditional techniques for sampling and handling research participants are almost impossible to use during or immediately following a disaster. In the case of predisaster interventions, it may be possible to assign participants randomly to intervention or nonintervention groups; however, it is still likely that it will be difficult or impossible to draw a random sample from a pre-existing list of eligible members of an affected population. The conditions and circumstances of disasters are simply too uncontrolled and unpredictable.

For example, access to the site of a disaster is often restricted. In some situations the site of a disaster may be dangerous, and data collection can therefore create significant personal risk. Federal, state, and local agencies are often preoccupied with managing the event, and may not be interested in talking with researchers (Seeger & Gouran, 2007). Often, emergency and disaster research is conducted a significant length of time after the event, when conditions have normalized; this requires respondents to answer questions about prior events, introducing issues of bias, or a number of types of retrieval error (Tourangeau, Rips, & Rasinski, 2002). Moreover, eliciting participation from people who have experienced considerable personal loss is difficult. These factors, among others, promote the use of some type of survey methodology.

Program evaluators are often comfortable with these methodological compromises, but concerns still arise. In disaster-response situations, having imperfect information is often seen as more desirable than having no information, especially when quick decisions must be made concerning the allocation of time, money, and personnel. Despite the methodological limitations imposed by the disaster scenario itself, when research and evaluation is reviewed and published in scholarly journals, it is often criticized for methodological issues related to data collection, randomization, and generalizability. This suggests a rift between the accepted standards of inference applied in academic circles and standards of evidence that make sense to disaster response organizations making decisions under conditions of extreme duress. Similarly, such concerns are sometimes raised by the funding agencies that determine the value of a program and whether that program will continue to receive funding. The reviewers of scholarly journals and program review committees are often not familiar with the conditions that confront disaster research.

Can applied empirical research and evaluation make a contribution to the knowledge of disasters, and if so, what are the opportunities and limitations? The current chapter first addresses the issues of data collection, randomization, and data analysis in crisis research. It outlines the difficulties of randomization, potential problems stemming from the absence of randomization, and potential corrections to these problems, and then addresses data analysis. This chapter posits that the responsible use of nonrandomized samples drawn from logical populations will produce data that are more valuable than randomized samples drawn from inappropriate populations. We further argue for the use of specific population frames, careful thought in selection of the unit of analysis, and the use of nonparametric statistical techniques as possible avenues for overcoming challenges associated with imperfect samples. We conclude by arguing that academic scholars studying the nature of crises must rethink the meaning of data and findings within the context of methods employed in order to avoid the erroneous dismissal of useful research.

Data Collection

Why Randomize? The advantages of the randomization of research participants are well documented. It is the best way to control for initial differences between the treatment and control group, both for variables that have been documented to confound the research outcome and for those variables unknown to the researcher or as yet undiscovered in the literature. Under perfect conditions of randomization, within-group variance should be consistent from group to group. The social science literature is filled with research outlining the limitations associated with techniques such as matching, regression, econometric simultaneous modeling, latent-variable modeling, and other techniques that seek to correct for initial differences and selection bias in nonrandomized studies. One of the strongest examples of the benefits of randomization comes from Sawilowsky (2007). In a series of experiments designed to examine differences in errors, three studies were completed with the goal of demonstrating what happens in commonly used quasiexperimental designs. Results demonstrated several potential errors that manifest when using nonrandomized designs, most notably increases in Type 1 errors.

Although many arguments have been made against nonrandomized designs, Sawilowsky provides possibly the strongest case for the superiority of randomization. The current authors, however, disagree with the claim that there is no place in science for nonrandomized designs. As noted by Campbell and Stanley (1963), nonrandomized designs are useful in situations where better designs are not feasible (see also Shadish, Cook, & Campbell, 2002). Moreover, Anderson et al. (1980) listed the following reasons for conducting nonrandomized experiments. They suggest their use when it might be unethical to assign the treatment randomly. Further, they may be advantageous when it is not logistically possible to conduct a randomized study, and when a randomized study might be prohibitively expensive.

Disaster research in particular is a context in which a strong argument can be put forth that nonrandomized designs are acceptable. Although it is well documented that purely academic research rewards studies that are stable and highly controlled, the applied context of field disaster research introduces a myriad of social, environmental, cultural, political, and legal variables that simply cannot be controlled by the researcher. Furthermore, under these conditions applied researchers are more than likely seeking data that pertain directly to a particular incident; in the absence of perfect control, they will favor data that is drawn from ecologically relevant conditions.

Despite arguments in favor of nonrandomized samples under certain conditions, academics often criticize crisis research for reliance on non-random samples when conducting survey research. The argument typically revolves around the question of validity. In academic journals, many reviewers adhere to the belief that if a sample design does not use some type of randomization it is fatally biased. This belief remains despite the fact that the inability to obtain a random sample and to assign participants to treatment and control groups randomly is common in social and behavioral science research. Researchers are frequently permitted access to various settings for research purposes, only to find that the treatment and control groups available must be limited to intact groups. The same is true for disaster researchers. More often than not, it is logistically impossible to obtain a population list from which participants may be randomly selected. Given the difficulties associated with gaining access to those affected by disasters, researchers may be limited in only having access to an intact group of people affected by a disaster, often located within a shelter or relief organization.

Obviously crisis research is not experimental; disaster survey research is closer to quasiexperimental design in that there is less support for counterfactual inferences, forcing the researcher to enumerate alternative explanations to decide which are plausible. Regardless, the belief that samples are biased because of the unfeasibility of random selection and assignment is often voiced in reviews of crisis research. Several steps can be taken to strengthen the validity of the measures in the absence of randomization.

Research Design. As discussed, it is often not possible or desirable to randomize respondents when collecting data after a disaster. Because of this limitation researchers need to define their target population of interest carefully, and analyze the collected data accordingly (Groves et al., 2004). In a series of studies after Hurricane Katrina (see Lachlan, Burke, Spence, & Griffin, 2009; Lachlan & Spence, 2007; Lachlan, Spence, & Eith, 2007; Spence, Lachlan & Burke, 2007; Spence, Lachlan, & Griffin, 2007) nonrandomized designs were used. Access to displaced individuals after Katrina was difficult to obtain. Following the evacuation of New Orleans, many Katrina evacuees initially stayed in temporary housing. Homeless and in need of proper shelter, they were relocated to different parts of the country. In the immediate days following the evacuation, the acquisition of an accurate sampling frame was unrealistic; moreover, such lists did not exist. For the study, self-administered surveys were given to individuals in temporary relief shelters in more than five states. Although individuals of all income levels, races, and other important characteristics were represented in such shelters, the authors defined their target population as displaced residents of the New Orleans metropolitan area living in temporary relief shelters. An argument could be made that the experiences of the participants were directly generalizable to all displaced persons from Hurricane Katrina. Additionally, the demographic makeup of the sample closely resembled census data, and, through narrowing the definition of the target population, the lack of randomization became a smaller issue. By making appropriate caveats, acknowledging the limitations, and conducting additional evaluation of the data, applied researchers can make convincing arguments for the utility and validity of the findings. Providing a clear statement of assumptions and limitations allows the reader to assess the value, merit, significance, and potential utility of findings and conclusions.

Another approach to the research design is to change the unit of analysis in order to obtain a randomized sample (see Glendening, 1977; Sawilowsky, 2007). Therefore, if it is possible to shift the unit from the individual to a group, randomization becomes possible. This is contingent on the research question and the defined population. For example, if examining specific responses or needs after a tornado, the unit of analysis could be cities. If the tornado was large enough to cause damage to a large geographic area, all affected cities could be the population; cities could then be randomly selected. This does, however, potentially create other problems with composition of the selected groups.

An important issue involved with changing the unit of analysis is the use of individual scores rather than a unit mean. When changing the unit of analysis to cities (to stay with our previous analysis), the researcher must avoid the temptation to use individual scores rather than city means as the statistical unit of analysis (see Blair et al., 1983). Imagine an evaluator is examining the effectiveness of a statewide mitigation program after a tornado. He/she looks at the city as the unit of analysis and randomly selects 9 cities. If 900 individuals were surveyed from those cities the temptation to analyze with 899 degrees of freedom is likely rather than using 8 degrees of freedom. However, as noted by Blair, Higgins, Topping, and Mortimer (1983), this decision has the possibility of creating inflated Type I errors (especially when the t test is being used) and is theoretically inconsistent with the decision to randomize at the group level. Thus, even when a change in the unit of analysis is made in order to allow for randomization, care must be taken in the analysis.

Still another option is to attempt a census. Spence, Lachlan, McIntyre, and Seeger (2009) first did a random selection of radio stations in the United States with the goal of examining station preparedness for disasters. A follow-up study was completed after the Midwest flooding of 2008 (Spence, McIntyre, Lachlan, & Seeger, 2009). A flood map was used to identify all affected counties, and from there a list of every radio station that broadcasts to the affected counties was created. That list was compared with the database of all broadcast stations as identified by the Federal Communication Commission. After all stations that broadcast to the affected areas were identified, self-report surveys were mailed out to each station. Randomization was therefore not a concern. However, even with a potential census, threats may manifest. In the follow-up study, issues of nonresponse bias emerged, because 60% of the surveys were returned. Thus, even when care is taken, threats to the data can emerge. As with all research, it comes back to trade-offs. Threats appear; therefore, minimizing such threats is more important to data quality and use than is randomizing the sample.

Data Analysis. In the absence of randomization, the statistical assumptions associated with inferential statistics are often violated. However, these violations also are evident in randomized experiments, yet rarely addressed. Given the departure from such assumptions attributed to the difficulty of data collection before, during, and after disasters, researchers should correct for the violations of these assumptions by using appropriate statistical analyses. Nonparametric methods have the benefit of requiring fewer statistical assumptions, thus they are able to preserve Type I error rates to nominal alpha when testing hypotheses without making an appeal to population parameters.

Tests of significance and comparisons of means are popular statistical tools in disaster research. Although the t test is ripe with advantages and has a long history of use in the social sciences, it can be quite nonrobust, especially when certain parameters have been violated (Sawilowsky & Blair, 1992). One such parameter is the deviation from a normal distribution caused by a nonrandomized sample. This next section provides a brief discussion of the advantages of the Wilcoxon rank-sum Mann–Whitney U test (Mann & Whitney, 1947; Wilcoxon, 1945) over the t test for independent samples and provides suggestions for those in disaster research.

Many statistical tests are based upon the assumption that the data are sampled from a Gaussian distribution; whereas in practice this is not often the case. A normal probability plot can be used to assess whether the distribution is Gaussian; alternatively, researchers can use one of a number of tests to determine the properties of a sample, most notably the Kolmogorov–Smirnov test of normality. The Kolmogorov–Smirnov test is better at testing normality than chi-square, but it is limited and needs an adjustment called Lillifore's test. Therefore, simply looking at the distribution should be adequate to determine the distribution shape. A vast body of research supports the notion that normality-assuming statistics may be relatively nonrobust in the presence of non-Gaussian distributions (see Blair, 1981; Micceri, 1989).

In most situations for disaster researchers, parametric and nonparametric tests of significance will produce similar or near similar results, with nonparametric statistics having more robust properties. However, by using the Wilcoxon–Mann–Whitney (WMW) instead of Student's t test, or Kruskal–Wallis (1952) instead of ANOVA, the researcher and evaluator can use a counterargument against the notion that an error in the data analysis has occurred due to a violation of the normality assumption.

As is the case with many other fields of behavioral science, the most common test for two independent samples is Student's t test. This can be used in disaster research to compare groups, such as survivors versus the general public. Disaster researchers, particularly with an interest in emergency communication or disaster mitigation, are often concerned with research questions exploring the differences between two groups. Essentially the question of what worked for some and did not work for others drives much of this research. The concern, particularly for academic researchers, who may be married to the use of traditional inferential procedures, is that the two groups may differ on much more than their response to the disaster. There may be a wide variety of differences between the groups, and the homogeneity of variance assumption on the dependent variable under observation may also not hold.

The t test on independent samples assumes that the two populations are normal with identical variances, whereas the WMW does not rest on assumptions of the sample distributions. Again, this is advantageous to crisis researchers, who may be unlikely to obtain a true randomized sample. It is often argued that the t is robust to deviations for populations from a normal distribution, and is more powerful than nonparametric counterparts and that the t is robust with respect to Type I errors (Boneau, 1960, 1962).

The t test and WMW have nearly equivalent power, with perhaps a small advantage going to the t test insofar as Type I errors are concerned, *provided* there is a normal distribution, equality between group sizes, larger sample sizes, and that the test is two tailed (Bradley, 1968; Hodges & Lehmann, 1956; Lehmann, 1975). However, when normality is violated, sample sizes are smaller, and group sizes are not equivalent; as a statistical test the WMW can be three–four times as powerful (Blair, Higgins, & Smitely, 1980). Many of the previous characteristics are typical of disaster samples. The power advantages of nonparametric measures increase with sample size for low to midlevel parts of the t test's power spectrum.

A common source of confusion exists on when to use the t or the WMW. Some researchers opt to use the WMW test only when testing for shift in location. Although acceptable, the WMW is advantageous in other circumstances. Others perform both the t test and the WMW, and accept the WMW only if it rejects the null and the t does not; however, there is no justification for this decision and it leads to an increase in experiment-wise Type I error. (See Sawilowsky, 2005, for an extended discussion on factual or inaccurate reasons for choosing the t.) Finally, many are oblivious to the research findings of the past quarter century (Blair & Higgins, 1980; Sawilowsky & Blair, 1992), and simply ignore the WMW test in favor of the t test. Others may not even know of its existence.

Several factors should be examined in choosing either the t or WMW. One consideration is the population distribution and its departure from a Gaussian shape. If the distribution is nonnormal, one should consider using the WMW. A second factor is sample size. For smaller sample sizes the WMW has demonstrated more power than the t, and it is acceptable to choose the WMW in such a situation. Finally, when the groups are not equivalent, the WMW is the more appropriate choice. Thus, in the absence of randomization, choosing the WMW over the t does not solve the limitations created with a nonrandom design, but the use of this and other tests provide the researcher an argument about why in the absence of randomization, other considerations have been addressed. For example, Lachlan, Spence, and Seeger (2009) looked at respondents' levels of psychological distress on 9/11, in an attempt to see whether or not certain media-related coping behaviors were successful. Both an ad hoc examination of the dependent variables and a series of Kolmogorov–Smirnov tests revealed that the distributions of the distress scores were nonnormal. Thus, the authors reported WMW tests instead of t, despite the fact that both the parametric and nonparametric analyses produced similar findings.

Similarly the Kruskal–Wallis test (Kruskal & Wallis, 1952) can be used over ANOVA. The Kruskal–Wallis statistic is identical to a one-way ANOVA with the data replaced by their ranks. It is an extension of the WMW test to three or more groups and provides similar advantages. However, in situations where regression is needed, this becomes more difficult; many techniques that avoid the underlying assumption are tedious to compute.

Value of the Collected Data. It is apparent that there are arguments to consider concerning the practicality of obtaining data under extreme conditions, and analysis procedures that may control for some of the problems associated with these techniques. There is a more obvious argument in favor of nonrandomized techniques in disaster studies: face validity.

The "Science of Sophomores." Some would argue in favor of the random selection of participants. However, there may be trade-offs related to face validity that render random selection not ideal, especially when considering the meaning of the data itself. It is easy to select randomly when working with a sample of convenience. For example, when conducting experimental research within a university, one can simply randomly select from a list of available students, bring them into the laboratory, and randomly assign them to treatment groups. The applied researcher is likely more concerned with gaining access to individuals who have actually experienced some particular phenomenon, as opposed to readily available individuals who may be simply airing opinions of a phenomenon they have witnessed second- or third-hand. In appraising the value of data and its actual meaning, the obvious choice seems to be the minor sacrifice of randomization in favor of responses that are directly related to the disaster under consideration. A nonrandomized sample of individuals who directly experienced a crisis will produce data far more valuable than a sample composed of participants from a university, who received extra credit in a course for participation in a study in which they were asked to appraise an indirect experience.

One consideration often overlooked in sampling and randomization is the consideration of the population to whom the sample is to generalize. For example, if one wants to find out what went wrong during a disaster-response phase that led to displacement, a sample of displaced individuals is appropriate. Randomized or not, this is a better sampling strategy than drawing from all members of a geographic area, a random sample of the general population, or worst of all, college students who happen to be on hand and readily available to offer ad hoc opinions about scenarios with which they have no experience.

Furthermore, even in instances in which random assignment is performed on a representative sample and subjects are randomly assigned to both treatment and control groups, there are validity threats that accompany random assignment, particularly in field settings. Often overlooked is the notion of subject preference (McCall & Green, 2004). Because it is difficult to keep subjects blind to the intention of a field study, they may become aware of different conditions and demonstrate a preference for one over the other. For example, consider a group that receives some sort of mitigation intervention and another does not; those in the control group would strongly prefer to receive the intervention. Their forced inclusion in the control group will bias their responses. It also leads to a process known as resentful demoralization (Bickman & Reich, 2008), where participants may not perform an assigned task or give up on the procedure because they feel neglected. Even if these internal-validity threats related to randomization do not occur, Berk (2005) reminds us that randomized control groups—often held as the gold standard in research design—are no more immune to external validity threats than any other design, particularly if the procedure in question departs from an ecologically valid experience.

Despite this, the social sciences are littered with studies drawn from pure convenience samples of available participants. Academic researchers accept convenience samples utilizing random assignment as viable, while vilifying field samples that, if nothing else, at least examine the population in question. The issue is the value of the data. A nonrandomized sample collected after a disaster, with a specific target population, is more valuable than resorting to the convenience of college students. The frequent use of students as a sample has created a genre of research labeled the "science of the sophomore" (Sears, 1986). Moreover, an argument could be made that most experimental research does not truly randomize participants. Although outside the scope of this chapter, it could be further argued that almost the entire body of experimental research in the social sciences has been drawn from samples that are more flawed than nonrandomized field samples.

Conclusion

This chapter has attempted to address some of the problems and challenges facing crisis and disaster researchers and program evaluators and propose a number of techniques for dealing with these challenges, both in terms of generating data and in terms of interpreting data. Because crises are by definition nonroutine and unexpected, they present a condition that forces the applied researcher to think outside of the conventions of social scientific inference. Unpredictable circumstances may necessitate the use of atypical practices in terms of design, data collection, and analysis, and certain conventions concerning collection and analysis may be called into question. We would argue, however, that there are certain practices that may help the researcher in ensuring data quality and reasonable scientific inference when violating these conventions. In fact, we would further contend that many standing conventions actually pose limits to social science inference, not to mention evaluating disaster management response efforts. Regardless, our position is that the careful uses of nonrandomized samples drawn from appropriate sampling frames are more valuable than randomized samples drawn from inappropriate populations. We further argue that in the absence of perfect randomization procedures, the use of nonparametric statistical inference may insulate the researcher from certain criticisms and present the data in a compelling and scientifically valid way. Finally, we have made the argument that careful consideration of the meaning and context of data may help prevent scholars from erroneously dismissing this data as invalid. It is our hope that these arguments encourage further debate and a careful reexamination of the methods typically employed in research during and following crises and disasters.

References

Anderson, S., Auquier, A., Hauck, W., Oakes, D., Vandaele, W., & Weisberg, H. I. (1980). *Statistical methods for comparative studies: Techniques for bias reduction*. New York: Wiley.

Berk, R. A. (2005). Randomized experiments as the bronze standard. *Journal of Experimental Criminology, 1*, 417–433.

Bickman, L., & Reich, S. M. (2008). Randomized control trials: A gold standard with feet of clay. In S. Donaldson, T. C. Christie, & M. M. Mark (Eds.), *What counts as credible evidence in applied research and evaluation?* Thousand Oaks, CA: Sage.

Blair, R. C. (1981). A reaction to "Consequences of failure to meet assumptions underlying the fixed effects analysis of variance and covariance." *Review of Educational Research, 51*, 499–507.

Blair, R. C., & Higgins, J. J. (1980). A comparison of the power of Wilcoxon's rank-sum statistic to that of Student's *t* statistic under various nonnormal distributions. *Journal of Educational Statistics, 5*, 309–335.

Blair, R. C., Higgins, J. J., & Smitely, W.D.S. (1980). On the relative power of the *U* and *t* tests. *British Journal of Mathematical and Statistical Psychology, 33*, 114–120.

Blair, R. C., Higgins, J. J., Topping, M.E.H., & Mortimer, A. L. (1983). An investigation of the robustness of the *t* test to unit of analysis violations. *Educational and Psychological Measurement, 43*, 69–80.

Boneau, C. A. (1960). The effects of violations of assumptions underlying the *t* test. *Psychological Bulletin, 57*, 49–64.

Boneau, C. A. (1962). A comparison of the power of the *U* and *t* tests. *Psychological Review, 69*, 246–256.

Bradley, J. V. (1968). *Distribution-free statistical tests*. Englewood Cliffs, NJ: Prentice-Hall.

Campbell, D. T., & Stanley, J. C. (1963). *Experimental and quasi-experimental designs for research*. Chicago: AERA.

Glendening, L. K. (1977). *Operationally defining the assumption of independence and choosing the appropriate unit of analysis.* Unpublished doctoral dissertation, Michigan State University, East Lansing.

Groves, R. M., Fowler, F. J., Couper, M. P., Lepkowski, J. M., Singer, E., & Tourangeau, R. (2004). *Survey methodology.* Hoboken, NJ: Wiley.

Hodges, J. L., & Lehmann, E. L. (1956). The efficiency of some nonparametric competitors of the *t*-test. *The Annals of Mathematical Statistics, 27,* 324–335.

Kruskal, W. H., & Wallis, W. A. (1952). Use of ranks in one-criterion variance analysis. *Journal of the American Statistical Association, 47,* 583–621.

Lachlan, K. A., Burke, J. M., Spence, P. R., & Griffin, D. (2009). Risk perceptions, race, and Hurricane Katrina. *The Howard Journal of Communication, 20,* 295–309.

Lachlan, K. A., & Spence, P. R. (2007). Hazard and outrage: Developing a psychometric instrument in the aftermath of Katrina. *Journal of Applied Communication Research, 35,* 109–123.

Lachlan, K. A., Spence, P. R., & Eith, C. (2007). Access to mediated emergency messages: Differences in crisis knowledge across age, race, and socioeconomic status. In R. S. Swan & K. A. Bates (Eds.), *Through the eye of Katrina: Social justice in the United States* (pp. 203–220). Durham, NC: Carolina Academic Press.

Lachlan, K. A., Spence, P. R., & Seeger, M. (2009). Terrorist attacks and uncertainty reduction: Media use after 9/11. *Behavioral Sciences of Terrorism and Political Aggression, 1*(2), 101–110.

Lehmann, E. L. (1975). *Nonparametrics.* San Francisco: Holden-Day.

Mann, H. B., & Whitney, D. R. (1947). On a test of whether one of two random variables is stochastically larger than the other. *Annals of Mathematical Statistics, 18,* 50–60.

McCall, R. B., & Green, B. L. (2004). Beyond the methodological gold standards of behavioral research: Considerations for practice and policy. *Society for Research in Child Development Social Policy Report, 18*(2), 3–19.

Micceri, T. (1989). The unicorn, the normal curve, and other improbable creatures. *Psychological Bulletin, 105,* 156–166.

Sawilowsky, S. S. (2005). Misconceptions leading to choosing the *t* test over the Wilcoxon–Mann–Whitney test for shift in location parameter. *Journal of Modern Applied Statistical Methods, 4,* 598–600.

Sawilowsky, S. S. (2007). ANCOVA and quasi-experimental design: The legacy of Campbell and Stanley. In S. S. Sawilowsky (Ed.), *Real data analysis* (pp. 213–238). Charlotte, NC: Information Age.

Sawilowsky, S. S., & Blair, R. C. (1992). A more realistic look at the robustness and type II error properties of the *t* test to departures from population normality. *Psychological Bulletin, 111,* 352–360.

Sears, D. O. (1986). College sophomores in the laboratory: Influence of a narrow data base on social psychology's view of human nature. *Journal of Personality and Social Psychology, 51,* 515–530.

Seeger, M., & Gouran, D. (2007). Introduction to special issue on the 2005 Atlantic hurricane season. *Journal of Applied Communication Research, 25,* 1–8.

Shadish, W. R., Cook, T. D., & Campbell, D. T. (2002). *Experimental and quasi-experimental designs for generalized causal inferences.* Boston: Houghton Mifflin.

Spence, P. R., Lachlan, K. A., & Burke, J. M. (2007). Adjusting to uncertainty: Coping strategies among the displaced after Hurricane Katrina. *Sociological Spectrum, 27,* 653–678.

Spence, P. R., Lachlan, K. A., & Griffin, D. (2007). Crisis communication, race and natural disasters. *Journal of Black Studies, 37,* 539–554.

Spence, P. R., Lachlan, K. A., McIntyre, J. J., & Seeger, M. (2009). Serving the public in a crisis: Radio and its unique role. *Journal of Radio and Audio Media, 16*(2), 144–159.

Spence, P. R., McIntyre, J. J., Lachlan, K. A., & Seeger, M. (2009). *Flooding in the heartland: How the radio industry responded.* Unpublished manuscript, Western Michigan University, Kalamazoo, MI.

Tourangeau, R., Rips, L. J., & Rasinski, K. (2002). *The psychology of survey response.* London: Cambridge University Press.

Wilcoxon, F. (1945). Individual comparisons by ranking methods. *Biometrics, 1,* 80–83.

Patric R. Spence is an assistant professor in the School of Communication at Western Michigan University.

Kenneth A. Lachlan is an associate professor of sociology and director of the Communication Studies program at the University of Massachusetts Boston.

9

Evaluation of Disaster and Emergency Management: Do No Harm, But Do Better

Liesel Ashley Ritchie, Wayne MacDonald

Abstract

*The authors identify key issues for the improvement of evaluations of disaster
and emergency management. The value of an interagency approach is discussed,
as is the importance of the crossover lessons from international and domestic
evaluation efforts. The authors discuss specific ways evaluation is tied to
the larger context of guidelines and standards in humanitarian assistance.*
© Wiley Periodicals, Inc., and the American Evaluation Association.

Evaluating disaster and emergency assistance is an emerging focus in
evaluation, an extension and refinement of development activity with
a longer history. Working in the highly charged environment of a
large-scale disaster can be difficult and dangerous. In extreme situations,
evaluators are exposed to risks to their safety as they attempt to do their
work.

Difficult and dangerous though it may be to conduct an evaluation of
disaster assistance either during a relief effort or soon after, it is a critical
component of emergency management. Without assessing the effectiveness
of aid, funders, providers, and people on the ground will be unable to make

informed decisions about efficient delivery of assistance in the current crisis, or learn lessons in anticipation of the next disaster. Past decisions and future plans on any aspect of relief efforts will inevitably impact the outcomes of other aspects. And these all happen within the context of social, demographic, cultural, political, legal, environmental, and technological challenges.

Evaluation findings, when credible and properly understood, can influence policy directly related to protecting and saving lives. This makes it critical to complete evaluations in a timely fashion, since results will affect the provision of services when lives are at stake.

Internationally, assessing the effectiveness, efficiency, and impact of humanitarian assistance has increased over the past 20 years from a handful of evaluations in the early 1990s to a situation where the Active Learning Network for Accountability and Performance in Humanitarian Action (www.alnap.org) has now catalogued many hundreds of evaluations. But experience at the international level has not translated so well to the national level. There is a clear movement internationally toward interagency and systemwide evaluation efforts. This strategic momentum shows promise for maximizing limited resources, enhancing the explanatory power of evaluation, increasing potential for obtaining useful information, and then delivering it to those who need it in a timely fashion.

But domestically, this systemwide assessment strategy is still in its infancy as demonstrated, for instance, by the response to Hurricane Katrina in the United States. The absence of a single stakeholder in the health and nutrition sector, for example, with overall authority for evaluation policy implementation and control of resources, adds to the complexity of evaluation efforts in that arena. Lessons learned from these efforts demonstrate the need to strengthen technical issues and governance, critical to advancing future evaluation efforts.

A coordinated evaluation strategy requires the inclusion of affected populations throughout the process. But ensuring that affected populations, whether viewed as victims, survivors, or beneficiaries, are appropriately involved requires persistence on the part of investigators. It takes more than lip service. The time has come for more concerted efforts on this front. It will take considerable effort to establish community ties and capabilities in advance of a crisis, where that's possible, or quickly after the onset of a disaster.

If we consider evaluation experience in this arena as a continuum, with the most experience on one end and the least experience on the other, there is much distance between those operating internationally and those working exclusively with a national context. There is a critical need for direct communication and the sharing of experiences among international and national organizations and individuals engaged in disaster and emergency evaluation.

Evaluation lessons following Hurricane Katrina, not to mention preparedness and response, could have been better informed by previous work in the global context. This is not to say that those operating in the international arena have mastered every issue. Rather, they are faced with many methodological challenges and so are more aware of potential pitfalls and solutions. Moreover, there may be things that those working internationally can learn from others with a fresh perspective—things they may have learned long ago, but now take for granted.

Evaluation Activities Informed by Humanitarian Assistance Standards

Not surprisingly, but worth noting, a number of evaluation issues are connected to international humanitarian standards and guidelines. Several independent agencies came together to further develop emergency response standards in the aftermath of the multiagency evaluation, *The International Response to Conflict and Genocide: Lessons from the Rwanda Experience* (Steering Committee of the Joint Evaluation of Emergency Assistance to Rwanda, 1996). Indeed, the Rwanda genocide was a watershed event for many aspects of humanitarian strategy and tactics. Among the advances were the Good Humanitarian Donorship Initiative, The Sphere Project, ALNAP, the Inter-Agency Network for Education in Emergencies, and the Humanitarian Accountability Partnership. Coalitions created to improve emergency response such as the Inter-Agency Standing Committee, the Emergency Capacity Building Project, the Tsunami Evaluation Coalition, and the Clinton NGO Impact Initiative also collaborated on elaborating guidelines to enhance their effectiveness. The current disaster in Haiti will be a test of what has been learned in the past ten years about coalitions' roles in disaster response and evaluation.

Less evident is the extent to which these various standards may be used in designing and implementing evaluations. There is little doubt that evaluation codes of conduct intersect with those of humanitarian organizations. Independence, neutrality, and impartiality are a few themes coincidental to disaster response and evaluation. Evaluators will continue to draw on these and other established standards to frame needs assessment, monitoring, and evaluation activities both internationally and domestically with the aim of achieving a more responsive approach.

In the United States and other national jurisdictions, efforts to develop standards and guidelines are lagging, leaving the various U.S. sectors behind those with more exposure to and experience with mass disasters. This may be largely attributed to the fact that the United States and Western European countries have not encountered disasters on the scale of those faced by many other nations. But in the aftermath of 9/11 and Hurricanes Katrina and Rita, the learning curve steepened. The 2010 earthquake in Haiti is the most recent example. Evaluators are finding themselves in new territory. Many are seeking to address increased demands for transparency, accountability, and learning in a variety of sectors concerned with disaster preparedness, response, and recovery. Evaluators must also navigate these traditional phases of disaster in relation to broader issues of community resilience.

Methodological Issues. In general, it is most important to focus on the type of evaluation approach used in the context of disaster and emergency management rather than prescribing certain methods. The most important evaluation approaches in disaster and emergency management are developmental, formative or real-time evaluation, and summative. The key emphasis is on the intended *use* of evaluation findings, and we believe that a utilization focus should drive methodological approaches. Arguably, the methodological issues associated with evaluation in disaster and emergency settings are similar to those in other situations. The case may also be made that these issues are heightened by contextual factors outlined above and discussed throughout this volume. Perhaps the most important lessons learned by evaluators has been that classical designs and approaches, such as experimental designs and survey methods, cannot be rapidly transferred and applied in disaster contexts without adjustment or consideration of social, developmental, and cultural context. With that said, the fact that there are significant challenges associated with conducting evaluations in the emergency and disaster arena is not an excuse for poorly designed evaluations or shoddy implementation. Rather, evaluators should acknowledge the methodological limitations, closely examine their implications within broad minimum and maximum standards, and work creatively to advance our efforts to attend to and address those shortcomings. Real-time evaluation (RTE) and efforts to modify standard data collection strategies like survey methods within the ever-changing context of disasters and emergencies are both examples of ways that evaluation methods are being adapted.

Increasing Access to Evaluation Results. In addition to increasing the quantum of evaluation activities during the various phases of disaster and emergency management, there has been an increase in access to and the use of evaluation results. Access to evaluation findings and reports has improved over the past several years, as a result of initiatives such as ALNAP. Not only are evaluation results and recommendations more readily available in the public domain through posting on the Web, but evaluations are collectively analyzed with policy and programming aims in mind. The implications are discussed in regular gatherings of evaluators and program practitioners, as evidenced, for example, in the creation of a topical interest group of the American Evaluation Association focusing specifically on disaster and emergency management evaluation. Moreover, evaluation products are more closely scrutinized in terms of technical quality through metaevaluation efforts. Pressure to post evaluation findings and to have explicit organization statements that disclose managements' responses to evaluation recommendations will continue to mount.

Conclusion

There is an old adage: "To know what you know, and to know what you don't know, is to know." Evaluation and monitoring of disaster relief can contribute to both what we know and what we don't know. Evaluation is a process that discerns what can be known with some certainty, and can help to provide a clear vision of targets for the future.

Reference

Steering Committee of the Joint Evaluation of Emergency Assistance to Rwanda. (1996). *The international response to conflict and genocide: Lessons from the Rwanda experience.* Retrieved February 6, 2010, from http://www.reliefweb.int/library/nordic/index.html

LIESEL ASHLEY RITCHIE *is assistant director for research at the University of Colorado's Natural Hazards Center.*

WAYNE MACDONALD *is director of Corporate Performance and Evaluation with Canada's Social Sciences and Humanities Research Council in Ottawa.*

NEW DIRECTIONS FOR EVALUATION • DOI: 10.1002/ev

INDEX

ORDER FORM SUBSCRIPTION AND SINGLE ISSUES

DISCOUNTED BACK ISSUES:

Use this form to receive 20% off all back issues of *New Directions for Evaluation*.
All single issues priced at **$23.20** (normally $29.00)

TITLE	ISSUE NO.	ISBN

Call 888-378-2537 or see mailing instructions below. When calling, mention the promotional code JBXND to receive your discount. For a complete list of issues, please visit www.josseybass.com/go/ndev

SUBSCRIPTIONS: (1 YEAR, 4 ISSUES)

☐ New Order   ☐ Renewal

U.S.	☐ Individual: $85	☐ Institutional: $256
CANADA/MEXICO	☐ Individual: $85	☐ Institutional: $296
ALL OTHERS	☐ Individual: $109	☐ Institutional: $330

Call 888-378-2537 or see mailing and pricing instructions below.
Online subscriptions are available at www.interscience.wiley.com

ORDER TOTALS:

Issue / Subscription Amount: $ _____

Shipping Amount: $ _____
(for single issues only – subscription prices include shipping)

Total Amount: $ _____

SHIPPING CHARGES:		
SURFACE	DOMESTIC	CANADIAN
First Item	$5.00	$6.00
Each Add'l Item	$3.00	$1.50

(No sales tax for U.S. subscriptions. Canadian residents, add GST for subscription orders. Individual rate subscriptions must be paid by personal check or credit card. Individual rate subscriptions may not be resold as library copies.)

BILLING & SHIPPING INFORMATION:

☐ **PAYMENT ENCLOSED:** *(U.S. check or money order only. All payments must be in U.S. dollars.)*

☐ **CREDIT CARD:**   ☐ VISA   ☐ MC   ☐ AMEX

Card number _____ Exp. Date _____

Card Holder Name _____ Card Issue # *(required)* _____

Signature _____ Day Phone _____

☐ **BILL ME:** *(U.S. institutional orders only. Purchase order required.)*

Purchase order # _____
                    Federal Tax ID 13559302 • GST 89102-8052

Name _____

Address _____

Phone _____ E-mail _____

Copy or detach page and send to: **John Wiley & Sons, PTSC, 5th Floor**
                                    989 Market Street, San Francisco, CA 94103-1741

Order Form can also be faxed to: **888-481-2665**

PROMO JBXND

JB JOSSEY-BASS™
▸ New and Noteworthy Titles in **Research Methods**

Research Essentials: An Introduction to Designs and Practices,
Stephen D. Lapan (Editor), MaryLynn T. Quartaroli (Editor), ISBN:
9780470181096, Paperback, 384 pages, 2009, $75.00.

Research Methods for Everyday Life: Blending Qualitative and
Quantitative Approaches
Scott W. VanderStoep, Deidre D. Johnson, ISBN: 9780470343531,
Paperback, 352 pages, 2009. $75.00.

Methods in Educational Research: From Theory to Practice
Marguerite G. Lodico, Dean T. Spaulding, Katherine H. Voegtle, ISBN:
9780787979621, Hardcover, 440 pages, April 2006, $75.00.

SPSS Essentials: Managing and Analyzing Social Sciences Data
John T. Kulas, ISBN: 9780470226179, Paperback, 272 pages, 2008, $45.00.

Quantitative Data Analysis: Doing Social Research to Test Ideas
Donald J. Treiman, ISBN: 9780470380031, Paperback, 480 pages, 2009.
$75.00

Mixed Methods in Social Inquiry
Jennifer C. Greene, ISBN: 9780787983826, Paperback, 232 pages, 2007,
$45.00.

Action Research Essentials
Dorothy Valcarel Craig, ISBN: 9780470189290, Paperback, 272 pages, 2009.
$45.00.

Designing and Constructing Instruments for Social Research and
Evaluation
David Colton, Robert W. Covert, ISBN: 9780787987848, Paperback, 412
pages, 2007, $55.00.

AEA members: Take advantage of your 20 percent discount on these
titles by ordering at (877) 762-2974 or www.josseybass.com or and
entering code AEAF9.

JB JOSSEY-BASS™
▸ New and Noteworthy Titles in **Evaluation**

Program Evaluation in Practice: Core Concepts and Examples for
Discussion and Analysis
Dean T. Spaulding, ISBN: 9780787986858, Paperback, 176 pages, 2008,
$40.00

Evaluation Essentials: Methods For Conducting Sound Research
Beth Osborne Daponte, ISBN: 9780787984397, Paperback, 192 pages, 2008,
$60.00.

Evaluation Theory, Models, and Applications
Daniel L. Stufflebeam, Anthony J. Shinkfield, ISBN: 9780787977658,
Hardcover, 768 pages, 2007, $70.00.

Logic Modeling Methods in Program Evaluation
Joy A. Frechtling, ISBN: 9780787981969, Paperback, 160 pages, 2007,
$48.00.

Evaluator Competencies: Standards for the Practice of Evaluation in
Organizations
Darlene F. Russ-Eft, Marcie J. Bober, Ileana de la Teja, Marguerite Foxon,
Tiffany A. Koszalka, ISBN: 9780787995997, Hardcover, 240 pages, 2008,
$50.00

Youth Participatory Evaluation: Strategies for Engaging Young People
Kim Sabo Flores, ISBN: 9780787983925, Paperback, 208 pages, 2007, $45.00

Performance Evaluation: Proven Approaches for Improving Program
and Organizational Performance
Ingrid J. Guerra-López, ISBN: 9780787988838, Paperback, 320 pages, 2008,
$45.00

AEA members: Take advantage of your 20 percent discount on these
titles by ordering at (877) 762-2974 or www.josseybass.com or and
entering code AEAF9.